THE Alaska
ADVENTURE BOOK

THE Alaska ADVENTURE BOOK

ALASKA ILLUSTRATED
ANCHORAGE, ALASKA

The Alaska Adventure Book wishes to extend special thanks to the National Park Service and the U.S. Fish and Wildlife Service for the extensive information, material and staff aid in preparing this publication and for their dedicated service in preserving Alaska's wilderness resources. Sincere thanks is also owing to Bob Snider, Mark Butler, Beth McKay, Ann and George Bryson, Glen and Regine Cassity, George Yates, John McKay, Tim Huffman, Bev Neuman, Sue Miskill, Brian Miskill, Peter Powers, John Fowler, Dave Grimes, Brett Coburn, Bob Olendorf, Gerry Aylett, Michael Owens, Scott Lepine, Mark Skok, George Heim, Jim Powell, Dan Dixon of the Alaska Department of Commerce, Debbie Briscoe of the Anchorage Convention and Visitor's Bureau, Brett Thomas and Brian Green of Timeframe, David Kelley of Computerland, Suzi Lee and the MacTypeNet staff, and the Alaska Division of Tourism.

Publisher: Kris Cassity
Managing Editor: Kevin Cassity
Design Consultant: David Whitelaw
Cover Design: Dave Freeman
Photo Editor: John Fowler
Cartography: (regional maps) Maureen Milner, Laura Larson; (state map) Randy Titchenal

Editorial Staff: Ann Bryson, Michael Burwell, Beth McKay, Tim Huffman, Dave Creekman, John Whiting, Yvonne Cassity, Buttons Brokovitch, Paul Todd.

Production and Design Assistance: Miye Schakne , Randy Yost, Cris Peterson, SST Typography & Design Group, MacTypeNet, Karen MacCullen.

Publishing Consultants: Mark Butler, Tom Hughes.
Production Consultant: Codra Enterprises.

Advertising: Rita Harmon, Dottie Brown, Gwen Erwin, George Heim, Rebeca Hettich, Sue Miskill, Wade Hampton Miller, Sue Crow.

Front Cover Photos: (top row) Brian Okonek/Alaska-Denali Guiding, Peter Olsen/Afognak Cabins, John Fowler; (bottom row) Chuck Ash/Hugh Glass Backpacking Co., (middle & right) John Fowler.
Back Cover Photos: (top row) Chuck Ash/Hugh Glass Backpacking Co., John Fowler, David Grimes; (middle row) David Grimes; (bottom row) John Fowler.
Half and Full Title Page Photos: John Fowler

Copyright 1987 The Alaska Adventure Book (TM). All rights reserved. No part of this publication may be reproduced, transmitted or stored in any manner without the prior written permission of Alaska Illustrated. Printed and bound in Korea by Dong-A Printing.

Published by Alaska Illustrated, 200 West 34th Avenue, Box 384, Anchorage, Alaska 99503, (907) 243-1286

Library of Congress Catalogue Card Number: 87-070492; ISBN 0-9617945-0-X

Contents

Introduction/Map   6

Southcentral   8
Anchorage - Kenai - Alaska Railroad Southbound - Kenai Fjords - Southcentral State Ferry - Valdez - Wrangell/St. Elias - Bears.

Interior   32
Alaska Railroad Northbound - Denali - Fairbanks - Aurora Borealis - Yukon/Charley Rivers - Birds - Yukon Flats - Tetlin - Kanuti - Nowitna - Koyukuk.

Arctic   50
Gates of the Arctic - Selawik - National Rivers - Kobuk - Noatak - Permafrost - Cape Krusenstern - Alaska's Natives - Arctic.

Western   66
Lake Clark - Togiak - Yukon Delta - Innoko - Musk Ox - Bering Land Bridge.

Southwest   78
Kodiak - Russian America - Becharof - Katmai - Aniakchak - The Aleutian Invasion - Alaska Peninsula - Izembek - Alaska Maritime - Volcanos.

Southeast   92
Southeast State Ferry - Sitka - Juneau - Glaciers - Glacier Bay - Klondike.

The Travel Pages   105

Bibliography/Credits   117

The naturalist John Muir expressed the opinion that ". . . no other part of the earth known to man surpasses Alaska in imposing and beautiful scenery." Alaska is not only a land of great beauty; it is also a land of unusual variation and contrast. Whatever your conception of this northern land, you have many surprises in store. Sage brush and sun scorched deserts well above the Arctic Circle, skies covered with birds in tropically bright plumage, mountains which would tower over the Himalayas if placed side by side, volcanic isles covered with lush green foliage jutting up from azure oceans, roaming herds of buffalo and fertile farmlands are a few of the seemingly unlikely scenes which you may discover.

Alaska is as vast as it is varied. Travel to the farthest reaches of the state can involve distances comparable to those of a trip across the continental United States. For ease of reference the state is generally divided into six regions: Southcentral, Interior, Arctic, Western, Southwest, and Southeast. The pages which follow are organized in this fashion, providing an overview of the geography, flora, fauna and cultures of each of these regions as well as suggested visitor activities.

Although there are many activities which require only a minimum of planning, a trip within Alaska may require somewhat more preparation than travel in other parts of the United States. Travel to remote areas often requires knowledgeable evaluation of unusual conditions. Failure to retain experienced and qualified guides or operators can expose you to unnecessary risks. A listing or advertisement in this publication does not constitute an endorsement of a guide, operator or other service provider. Always inquire about the qualifications, experience and safety record of your service provider before making travel plans.

This book has been a cooperative undertaking of many people from all parts of the state who have shared their knowledge and love of this land. On behalf of those whose efforts contributed to making this publication possible, please accept our best wishes for a pleasant visit.

Southcentral

Southcentral Alaska is the most traveled region of the state and home to about two-thirds of its population. Southcentral is a geographically diverse group of sub-regions tied together by road, railroad and ferry systems. The convenience, economy and variety of transportation options make Southcentral somewhat unique.

To the south the Gulf Coast forms a 650-mile arch taking in not only the continent's highest coastal mountains, but extensive glaciers, fjords, island-speckled bays, lush rain forests and abundant wildlife. Road and rail systems to coastal towns connect with state ferry routes running through the Gulf of Alaska and on to Southwest. Most of the Gulf Coast falls within the Chugach National Forest, the nation's second largest protected forest. Winters here are mild by comparison to those in the northern continental states and summers are comfortably cool and rainy.

The forested plateaus of the Kenai Peninsula with their popular road-accessible fishing lie to the north and west of the coastal mountains along the southern shore of Cook Inlet. The Anchorage bowl sits north of Kenai across Cook Inlet and houses the great majority of the state's population and commerce. Winter weather here is colder than on the coast but still quite mild. Summers are pleasantly warm and dry.

The Matanuska/ Susitna Valley with its vast boreal forests, extensive river and lake systems and record producing farmlands lies to the north and is connected to Anchorage by road and railroad. The climate here is comparable to Anchorage. The eastern highlands of the Talkeetna Mountains, the Copper River Basin and the Wrangell-St. Elias Mountains are all accessible by way of spartan road systems. This area has a continental climate with very low temperatures in the winter and high temperatures in summer.

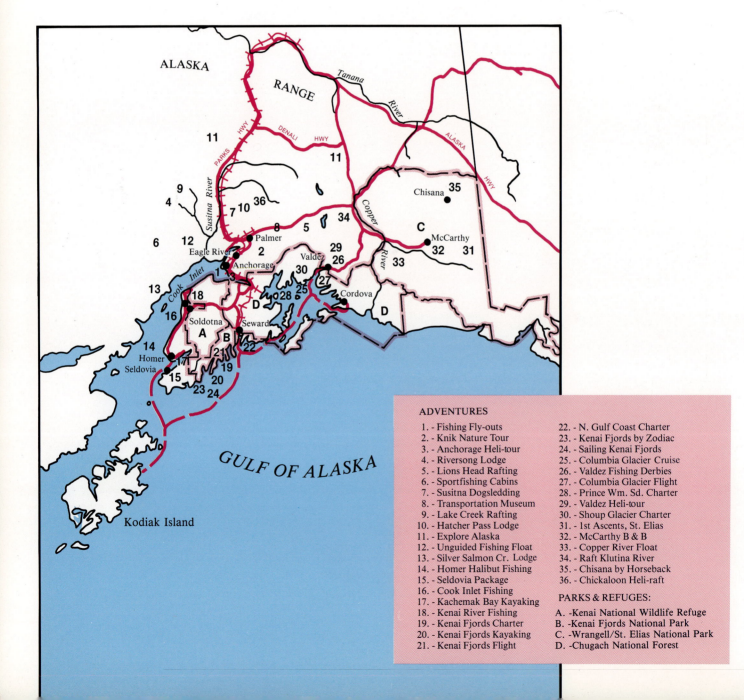

ADVENTURES

1. - Fishing Fly-outs
2. - Knik Nature Tour
3. - Anchorage Heli-tour
4. - Riversong Lodge
5. - Lions Head Rafting
6. - Sportfishing Cabins
7. - Susitna Dogsledding
8. - Transportation Museum
9. - Lake Creek Rafting
10. - Hatcher Pass Lodge
11. - Explore Alaska
12. - Unguided Fishing Float
13. - Silver Salmon Cr. Lodge
14. - Homer Halibut Fishing
15. - Seldovia Package
16. - Cook Inlet Fishing
17. - Kachemak Bay Kayaking
18. - Kenai River Fishing
19. - Kenai Fjords Charter
20. - Kenai Fjords Kayaking
21. - Kenai Fjords Flight
22. - N. Gulf Coast Charter
23. - Kenai Fjords by Zodiac
24. - Sailing Kenai Fjords
25. - Columbia Glacier Cruise
26. - Valdez Fishing Derbies
27. - Columbia Glacier Flight
28. - Prince Wm. Sd. Charter
29. - Valdez Heli-tour
30. - Shoup Glacier Charter
31. - 1st Ascents, St. Elias
32. - McCarthy B & B
33. - Copper River Float
34. - Raft Klutina River
35. - Chisana by Horseback
36. - Chickaloon Heli-raft

PARKS & REFUGES:

A. -Kenai National Wildlife Refuge
B. -Kenai Fjords National Park
C. -Wrangell/St. Elias National Park
D. -Chugach National Forest

Afternoon hike at 20-Mile River (John Fowler photo)

Anchorage

Anchorage (population 249,000) is the most visited destination in Alaska. Almost two thirds of the state's population lives in the vicinity of this commercial center of the state . Since Anchorage International Airport is a mid-point for several international air routes (the Europe/Asia route being the most heavily travelled) it is a stopover for some 4 to 5 million air passengers annually. By air Anchorage is 3 hours from Seattle, 5 hours from Los Angeles, 6 hours from Chicago, 7.5 hours from the East Coast, 7.5 hours from Tokyo and 9 hours over the pole from London.

Anchorage is located on a broad alluvial benchland which forms a wedge-shaped peninsula that extends from the base of the Chugach Mountains to the waters of Cook Inlet. The Chugach rise abruptly at the city's edge to an average elevation of 4000 to 5000 feet, with some peaks as high as 8000 to 10,000 feet. The half-million acre Chugach State Park--a hiker's delight--begins on the slopes of the Chugach literally at the municipal boundary. Including the Chugach, five mountain ranges are visible from the Anchorage bowl. These mountains provide both spectacular views and a climate sheltered from the Interior's cold winter weather and the Gulf of Alaska's wet summer storms.

Summer weather in Anchorage is dry (the area receives only 15 inches of precipitation annually) and comfortably warm. Highs average 60° F and temperatures in the 70's and 80's are not uncommon.

Winter weather in Anchorage is moderated not only by the surrounding mountains but also by the Pacific's Japanese current. During its coldest month (January) the city has average highs of 20°F. The Anchorage bowl receives an average 70 to 90 inches annual snowfall. The amount of snowfall increases significantly with moderate increases in elevation, extending the winter season by two months at the 1,000 to 2,000-foot elevation and making skiing possible in the Chugach year round. Because of its convenient location, favorable conditions and well-developed venues, Anchorage has secured the United States nomination to host the 1994 Winter Olympics.

Information: Anchorage Convention & Visitor's Bureau, 201 E. Third Avenue, Anchorage, AK 99501. (907) 274-3531, 276-4118. Anchorage Chamber of Commerce, 415 F Street, Anchorage, AK 99501.

Anchorage skyline from Cook Inlet (ACVB photo)

LAKE HOOD FISHING FLY-OUTS

Enjoy three full days of guided fly-out adventures from the Clarion, one of Anchorage's newest hotels, located next to Lake Hood at Lake Spenard. Each day's adventure is planned at breakfast based on where the weather is best, where the fish are biting, and where you want to go. You can fish all 5 species of salmon in the Kenai, Iliamna and Susitna drainages. Couples or groups wishing to fly out together and then split up for fishing and sightseeing can be easily accommodated. Those interested in wildlife observation can scan interesting situations from the sky, then land and take a closer look using spotting scopes. You'll return to the hotel each evening to relax and prepare for the next day's outdoor adventure. **June-Sept.**

Alaska Wilderness Travel. 121 W. Fireweed, Anchorage, AK 99503. (907) 277-7671, 1-800-544-2236.

KNIK GLACIER/LAKE GEORGE NATURE TOUR

Spend a half or a full day with bush pilot/guide, C. C. "Buck" Kuhn, Jr., on a glacier air tour and wildlife spotting expedition. Bring your camera and plenty of film. Normally you'll see Dall sheep, mountain goats, moose and sometimes bear. You'll fly over several spectacular glaciers. You'll land on sand/gravel bars along untamed rivers and at the base of glaciers so you can see the country close-up. At one of your landing sites, you'll enjoy a picnic consisting of Alaskan gourmet foods. Wilderness Air Tours offers a very personalized trip, custom designed for Grandma and Grandpa, Mom and Dad, or the kids. For the best ride and view, you will fly only when there is some blue sky and winds are light to variable. Tour limited to 3 persons. Ask about "no-fish, no-pay" guided fishing trips. **April-Oct.**

Wilderness Air Tours of Alaska. PO Box 770032, Eagle River, AK 99577. (907) 688-2478.

ANCHORAGE/CHUGACH STATE PARK HELICOPTER TOUR

Enjoy the geographical diversity of this region from the air. First, you'll heli-tour the city which is the proposed site of the 1994 Winter Olympics; then you'll continue along Turnagain Arm with its bore tides and jutting cliffs to Alyeska Ski Resort. Your flight then loops across Crow Creek Pass and through the peaks and glaciers of the Chugach mountain range. Landing on a glacier, you'll be treated to delicious Alaskan hors d'oeuvres and 15 minutes of alpine panorama in the nation's second largest state park. You will want to keep your eye out for moose, Dall sheep and bald eagles seen in this area. **Year Round.**

Alaska Wilderness Travel. 121 W. Fireweed, Anchorage, AK 99503. (907) 277-7671, 1-800-544-2236.

RIVERSONG LODGE, LAKE CREEK

Riversong Lodge is a very personalized fly-in lodge serving a maximum of twelve guests per week. Situated at the mouth of Lake Creek on the Yentna River, 65 air miles northwest of Anchorage, Riversong Lodge is known for its access to excellent salmon, trout, pike and grayling fishing June through September. During the winter, guests come to enjoy the solitude and cross-country skiing. The main lodge, built by hand from all native wood, offers rustic Alaskan charm in a comfortable setting. Your hosts, Carl and Kirsten Dixon, are known for their friendly hospitality, knowledge of the area, and home cooking so good that "Alaskan Passages" magazine devotes a monthly column to Kirsten's recipes. The garden provides the produce for hearty homestyle meals. Homemade bread and pastries are baked daily. **Year Round.**

Riversong Lodge. Skwentna, AK 99667. (907) 733-2931.

LION'S HEAD WHITEWATER RAFTING

On the International Whitewater Scale (class VI is maximum), Lion's Head rates class IV to V. Your day trip begins at Chickaloon Station, only an hour and a half's drive from Anchorage. After checking in, you'll take a bus ride through cottonwood and spruce forests into the high country of the upper Matanuska River with its excellent views of the Matanuska Glacier. Sheep are often sighted during the first several miles of smooth rafting down Caribou Creek and past the Matanuska glacial moraine. Then comes some of the best whitewater in Alaska--prepare to get wet. Upon emerging from the "Pearly Gates," your last big drop, you'll take a lunch break on the edge of the Matanuska Glacier. You can even go for a swim in a clearwater glacial "kettle" nearby. The river smooths out again for the last half of this 4-hour trip. **June-Sept.**

Alaska Wilderness Travel. 121 W. Fireweed, Anchorage, AK 99503. (907) 277-7671, 1-800-544-2236.

SPORTFISHING CABINS

Anchorage's Lake Hood, for many years the largest floatplane base in the world, is the major "jump-off" for remote fishing in Southcentral Alaska. Experienced professional pilots will fly you to a stream where the fish are biting. 22 wilderness cabins and framed wall tents are available. Depending on the season, you may try for salmon, grayling, rainbow trout and/or dolly varden. Camps are fully equipped with bunks, cooking and eating equipment and boat and motor where required. All fishing gear and bait is included. Watch moose, loons, ducks and beaver from a rustic, comfortable camp. Enjoy the view as your modern Cessna floatplane brings you and your catch back to town. **May-Sept.**

Alaska Wilderness Travel. 121 W. Fireweed, Anchorage, AK 99503. (907) 277-7671, 1-800-544-2236.

John Cooper

Jim Hudson

SUSITNA DOGSLEDDING

Meet some of the drivers and dogs who have mushed Alaska's historic 1,049-mile Iditarod Dogsled Race from Anchorage to Nome. Training camp is located 91 miles north of Anchorage on the Big Susitna River, under the watchful eye of Mt. Denali--called "The Great One" by Alaska's Athabascan Indians. Experience this vast, pristine wilderness as knowledgeable guides teach you to drive your own team. This area is an easy day trip from Anchorage and a couple of hours is plenty of time for picture taking and a taste of Alaskan hospitality. Overnighters and extended trips are also available. On these trips you'll travel with your guides to wilderness lodges or predetermined campsites in much the same way as early Alaskans. **Nov-March.**

Susitna Dog Tours. Box 404-G, Willow, AK 99688. (907) 495-6324, (800) 544-2235.

MUSEUM OF ALASKA TRANSPORTATION & INDUSTRY

The Museum of Alaska Transportation & Industry began near Palmer in 1976 with the acquisition of the remains of Anchorage's Transportation Museum of Alaska, which burned in 1973. The museum has grown to become an important part of Alaska's preservation, education and tourism effort. There are hundreds of exhibits covering air, sea, rail and land transportation, in addition to farming and mining. You can view the equipment, photographs and memorabilia which mark the development of transportation and industry in Alaska. You'll find it informative, interesting and entertaining. The 4.5-acre museum is located at mile 40.2 of the Glenn Highway, just outside of Palmer. Picnic tables and outdoor play equipment for children are available. Open 9-4 Tuesday through Saturday. **Year Round.**

Museum of Alaska Transportation & Industry. PO Box 909, Palmer, AK 99645. (907) 745-4493.

LAKE CREEK RAFTING

The crystal-clear waters of Lake Creek flow from the foothills of Denali (Mt. McKinley) 55 miles to the broad, glacier-fed Yentna River. Wildlife and birds are abundant in this drainage and the fishing is excellent in season. The trip begins from Anchorage with a flight-seeing tour of Denali and a floatplane landing on Chulatna Lake, at the headwaters of Lake Creek. You'll spend the days fishing, watching for wildlife, running the river, gathering berries, hiking and taking pictures. Along the way you'll have the opportunity to explore old trappers' cabins, watch for eagles nesting, and enjoy excellent views of Denali and the Alaska Range. Each night you'll enjoy a comfortable camp and your guides will prepare a delicious dinner. 4-8 day trips/5 days recommended. **June-Sept.**

Alaska River & Ski Tours, Inc. 1831 Kuskokwim St., Suite C, Anchorage, AK 99508. (907) 276-3418, Telex 25-147.

HATCHER PASS LODGE

Only one-and-a-half hours by road from Anchorage, Hatcher Pass Lodge is rich in history, scenic beauty and hospitality. From your own private cabin, nestled among mountain peaks, you can look out on the Matanuska Valley 3,000 feet below. After a day of hiking, enjoy a sauna perched over a creek and take a plunge into the "dipping hole." On your walk back to your cabin, stop by the main lodge restaurant and bar and sample a fondue, one of the house specialties. Over 50 varieties of wildflowers grow in the surrounding meadows, and Independence Mine State Historic Park is only a mile's walk away. The location is excellent both for hiking in the summer and cross-country skiing in the winter. The lodge offers a ski school in the winter. **Year Round.**

Hatcher Pass Lodge. Box 2655-F, Palmer, AK 99645. (907) 745-5897.

Don Svela

EXPLORE ALASKA ADVENTURE PACKAGE

This 13-day CampAlaska adventure package is a personalized, small-group tour for those who want to experience Alaska's many faces. Departing from Anchorage, you'll spend the first 3 days exploring Denali National Park. Continuing at a leisurely pace up the Denali Highway you'll visit the Yukon and Dawson City with its gold rush flavor and roaring twenties entertainment. From Dawson you'll canoe 130 miles to Eagle on the swift but placid Yukon River, enjoying its expansive vistas, wildlife, and historic relics. Crossing the Alaska Range, you'll take a treetop helicopter flight to the headwaters of the Chickaloon River for a thrilling day-and-a-half of whitewater. CampAlaska offers 15 flexible itineraries statewide, from 7 to 32 days, departing from Anchorage, Juneau and Seattle. Family tours available. **June-Sept.**

CampAlaska. PO Box 872247, Wasilla, AK 99687 (907) 376-9438.

ALEXANDER CREEK UNGUIDED FISHING FLOAT

Located near the base of Mt. Susitna (the "Sleeping Lady"), Alexander Creek is a gentle river, stretching only 25' in width and traveling at a leisurely 3-4 knots. After a fly-in over snow and glacier capped mountains, you'll spend five days floating downriver through a drainage known for its good salmon, trout, and grayling fishing. You'll enjoy watching for beaver and moose and will want to keep your eye out for signs of the black bear which frequent this area. In the evening, camp is made on streamside gravel beds and your dinner will be the succulent 'catch of the day.' Fish as late as you like; there's plenty of "midnight sun." **June-Sept.**

Alaska Wilderness Travel. 121 W. Fireweed, Anchorage, AK 99503. (907) 277-7671, 1-800-544-2236.

Photos by: (top) John Fowler; (middle and bottom) Sue Miskill.

Southcentral

Kenai
National Wildlife Refuge

The Kenai Refuge covers the western slopes of the Kenai Mountains and forested lowlands bordering Cook Inlet. The lowlands are composed of spruce and birch forests intermingled with hundreds of lakes. On the southeastern border of the refuge, the Kenai Mountains rise to more than 6,000 feet, presenting a barrier to the heavy rainfall of the Gulf Coast.

Turn of the century wildfires here left clearings where lush glades of aspen, birch and spruce saplings quickly grew. Moose flourished with this increased food supply. Over 9,000 moose now browse on refuge lands. The refuge is also host to Dall sheep, mountain goat (which reach their western limits here), coyote, brown and black bear, lynx, wolverine, beaver and small mammals. Caribou were reintroduced to the refuge after the Stone caribou herd was wiped out in the early 1900's by commercial hunters and forest fires that ravaged their lowland lichens food supply. Wolves disappeared from the Kenai Peninsula by the turn of the century due to zealous poisoning campaigns. However, they reappeared on the refuge in 1960. This recolonization is the only recent case of wolves expanding their range in North America.

The refuge is home to the continent's largest loon population, and trumpeter swans summer here. In all, 160 bird species have been recorded at the refuge.

Although the refuge is easily accessible from the Sterling Highway, fishing remains excellent. Four kinds of salmon spawn in refuge rivers and Kenai River king salmon are the largest in the world, with some running near 100 pounds. Lakes and streams hold lake trout, arctic char, dolly varden, kokanee, steelhead, grayling and whitefish. There are over 200 miles of established trails and water routes including the Swanson River and Swan Lakes canoe trails. Visitors can fly to remote lakes, take horse-pack trips into roadless areas, or float whitewater rivers. Developed facilities are available year-round for day and overnight camping.

Information: Refuge Manager, Kenai National Wildlife Refuge, PO Box 2139, Soldotna, AK 99669. (907) 262-7021.

Chickaloon River landing strip (John Fowler photo)

SILVER SALMON CREEK LODGE

The Silver Salmon Creek area has long been noted for its salmon, halibut and dolly varden fishing. Not as well known are the multitude of bird-watching opportunities, salt-water king salmon fishing and local fossil beds. Spring provides the solitude and extended daylight to enjoy the northern migration of sea and land birds, including trumpeter swans, bald eagles, puffins and sandhill cranes. Many of these birds nest in the immediate area and arrive in their striking mating plumage. Nearby is the Chisik Island Bird Sanctuary. At this fully modern lodge overlooking a beautiful coastal area of Cook Inlet, hearty meals are served home style. Visitors may also cook their meals in completely furnished guest cabins. A variety of services, including charters, are available and can be tailored to individual budgets. **May-Sept.**

Silver Salmon Creek Lodge. PO Box 3234, Soldotna, AK 99669. (907) 262-4839.

HOMER HALIBUT FISHING

Let your worries go in the invigorating spray of the Kachemak Bay salt air. Enjoy the beauty of unspoiled inlets and islands, framed by glacier-covered mountains and distant volcanoes. You'll see eagles, colorful puffins, sea otters, porpoises, seals, sea lions and whales in your quest for the largest fish you may ever catch. Your journey will begin on the 50' Sourdough or 43' Sea Witch. These powerful boats are known for their cleanliness, safety and state of the art electronics and equipment. Last year Homer Ocean Charters' clients won 2 out of 3 Homer fishing derbies, with scores of fish weighing in at over 100 lbs., and some as much as 300 lbs. Day charters are available or, for more serious fishing, one to two day safaris to remote fisheries where adventure is truly the name of the game. **May-Sept.**

Homer Ocean Charters, Inc. Box 2543, Homer, AK 99603. (907) 235-6212.

McKenzie

HISTORIC SELDOVIA / HALIBUT FISHING

Hop aboard a Cessna 207 in Anchorage for a spectacular flight along the glaciers of the Kenai Peninsula to the tiny picturesque fishing village of Seldovia, a former Russian fur-trading post. Comfortable, clean accommodations at the cozy new Annie McKenzie's Boardwalk Hotel on the waterfront give you a strategic view of fishing activities. On your first day you'll inspect the fishing fleet, beachcomb, watch the eagles and otters, walk bluffs and wooded trails, and visit the Russian Orthodox church. You'll top off the day at the sunset salmon bake. You'll spend your second day aboard one of the local charters fishing halibut in Kachemak Bay. **June-Aug.**

Alaska Wilderness Travel. 121 W. Fireweed, Anchorage, AK 99503. (907) 277-7671, 1-800-544-2236.

Rob Stapleton

COOK INLET SILVER SALMON FISHING

Pound for pound, the silver salmon is considered by many to be the scrappiest sportfish in the state. The Cook Inlet saltwater fishery offers quality 10-20 pound silvers and lots of them. This silver salmon sportfishing package is designed for persons who are flying to Alaska for a fast, action-packed trip and wish to maximize their fishing time. A 20-minute commuter flight from Anchorage will take you to the Kenai Peninsula. The package includes lodging, fishing equipment, airport transportation, Coast Guard licensed and insured guides, and the preparation, freezing and packaging of your catch for your return trip. Guests may also have their catch vacuum frozen, filleted, smoked, or canned. More that 50% of the guests on this trip are "returnees" from previous years. **June-Sept.**

Alaska Wilderness Travel. 121 W. Fireweed, Anchorage, AK 99503. (907) 277-7671, 1-800-544-2236.

KACHEMAK BAY KAYAK TOUR

Accessed via the city of Homer, Kachemak Bay is more than 200 square miles of coves, lagoons and bays. This setting is ideal for kayaking, hiking, fishing, crabbing, beachcombing, clamming, photography or just sightseeing. The Kenai Mountains, rising 3,000 feet above the bay, provide not only a spectacular backdrop for photographers, but a barrier to storms. This area is known for its good weather, with Homer enjoying more sunny days than any coastal city in Alaska. Your swift, stable 19-foot seacruising kayak makes it easy to get to the good fishing spots, put out shrimp and crab pots, or see otters, puffins and seals "up close and personal." Your guides will give you the opportunity to increase your comfort level in a kayak, help you understand and appreciate the flora and fauna of the bay, and provide old-fashioned good cooking. **May-Sept.**

Siwash Safaris. 2312 Loussac, Anchorage, AK 99517. (907) 248-0222.

KENAI RIVER KING SALMON FISHING

The Kenai River produced the current world record king salmon (97 lbs., 4 oz.) on May 17, 1985. You too can fish for the largest known strain of king salmon in the world. Johnson Brothers Guides and Outfitters will provide you with a registered professional fishing guide, a comfortable riverboat and all fishing equipment. Fish full or half days, only 30 minutes away from Anchorage by commuter airplane. Lodging is available for extended visits--Johnson Brothers recommends fishing 3 to 5 days. Getting there can be half the fun if you drive the Sterling Highway which passes through the beautifully forested Chugach Mountains. King salmon season runs **May 20 through July 31**. If you miss the kings, Johnson Brothers can show you excellent silver and pink salmon fishing in August and September.

Johnson Brothers Guides & Outfitters. 44526 Sterling Hwy., Soldotna, AK 99669. (907) 262-5357.

The Alaska Railroad
Southbound

This informal and comfortable state-owned line provides some of the state's most attractive and economical tour opportunities. During the summer a daily Whittier train leaves Anchorage in the morning on a two hour run which and travels along the edge of Turnagain Arm, between the Chugach and Kenai Mountains. At Portage the rail route leaves the Seward highway, travels up Portage Valley and tunnels over three and a half miles through the sheer rock cliffs of the Chugach Mountains to Whittier on Prince William Sound. Motorists wishing to make the connection with the State ferry in Whittier can take the Seward Highway to Portage and drive aboard flat cars for a half-hour shuttle to Whittier.

The railroad has recently added a summer passenger route from Anchorage to Seward on Resurrection Bay. This 4-5 hour trip traces the Anchorage-Whittier route as far as Portage and then splits off, traveling up the Placer Valley to Grandview Pass in the Kenai Mountains.

During the winter the railroad offers a charter to Grandview (through the Nordic Ski Club of Anchorage) for a day of superb backcountry skiing. The summer route continues from Grandview through the Kenai Mountains to Seward. This port provides access to Prince William Sound and Kenai Fjords National Park. The State ferry makes connections here to the Kodiak and the Prince William Sound routes.

Reservations on all routes are required, except on the vehicle shuttle between Portage and Whittier. The railroad also offers packaged trips which include fishing and sightseeing charters and overnight lodging in Whittier and Seward.

Information: Passenger Services, The Alaska Railroad, PO Box 107500, Anchorage, AK 99510. (907)265-2429 (Anchorage); (907)456-4155 (Fairbanks).

Southbound train on Turnagain Arm (John Fowler photo)

Southcentral

Kenai Fjords
National Park

Kenai Fjords National Park presents a striking interface between the glacial forces of the 300 square mile Harding Icefield, the geological forces of the crust of the Pacific Ocean floor, and the erosive forces of the waters of the Gulf of Alaska. The Harding, which sits atop the Kenai Mountains, is believed to be a remnant of a Pleistocene ice mass that once covered half the state of Alaska. It is sustained by 400 to 600 inches of annual snowfall. Almost half of its 36 glacial arms stretch toward the fjords of the Gulf. Sea stacks, islets and the sheer jagged shoreline of the fjords are actually remnants of mountains which were originally sculpted by Harding's ice.

The fjords are in a subduction zone where the North Pacific plate of the earth's crust is forcing its way under the North American plate, dragging down the edge of the Kenai peninsula in the process. From time to time a sudden slippage of these massive plates releases tremendous shock waves and can raise or lower the land by several feet. One such adjustment on March 27, 1964 was responsible for the great Alaska earthquake and dropped portions of the Kenai Fjords shoreline by over six feet in a three minute period.

A colony of four thousand sea lions inhabit coastal waters and untold centuries of "hauling out" here have worn the granite rock smooth. Twenty-two other marine mammal species, including porpoise, whale, dolphin, seal and sea otter also frequent the waters of this 587,000 acre park.

Visitors can reach the park by going first to Seward (by car, bus or railroad) or Homer (by car or plane) and then chartering a boat or plane into the park.

Information: Superintendent, Kenai Fjords National Park, PO Box 1727, Seward, AK 99664. (907) 271-4243.

Kayaking in Kenai Fjords at Pederson Lagoon (Brian Okonek photo/ Alaska-Denali Guiding)

John Fowler

KENAI FJORDS SIGHTSEEING CHARTER

Treat yourself to a day in Kenai Fjords National Park aboard the motor vessels "Kenai Fjords" or "Spirit", berthed in Seward. You'll see seals, sea otters, sea lion colonies and often a variety of whales. Ample time will be given for photographing wildlife and sea birds. Over 50 species of birds can be seen in the area, from bald eagles to puffins. One small island hosts over 20,000 horned and tufted puffins. You'll enter the park near Bear Glacier, travel through Cheval Narrows, round Aialik Cape and follow the coastline of Aialik Bay, arriving at a tidewater glacier by noon. There you can see ice calving from the glacier and hear the clinking of small ice bits around the vessel. You will then visit the Chiswell Island kittiwake rookery, with its Stellar sea lion colony and hosts of common murres rafting the waves or lining the sheer cliffs. **May-Sept.**

Kenai Fjords Tours. Box 1889AA, Seward, AK 99664. (907) 224-8068 or 224-3668.

KENAI FJORDS KAYAKING

At the southern end of the Kenai Peninsula, east of Homer, lies the rugged and scenic Kenai Fjords National Park with its hemlock and spruce forests, volcanic beaches, glaciers and sea cliffs. This area offers paddling opportunities at the face of tidewater glaciers. You'll feel as if you've gone back to the last ice age as you paddle among seal-laden ice floes from the Harding Icefield--one of the largest icefields in the United States. There is plenty of time to explore, to fish spawning streams for salmon and to observe the many varieties of bird and marine life abundant in this area. The quiet, maneuverable kayak provides an effective means of getting close to sea otters, seals, seabirds and, on occasion, porpoises and whales. **June-Sept.**

Ageya Kayak Tours. 2517 Foraker Dr., Anchorage, AK 99517. (907) 248-7140.

KENAI FJORDS & HARDING ICE FIELD FLIGHTSEEING

Kenai Fjords National Park is a truly unspoiled wilderness with crystal clear waterfalls and rugged terrain that teems with wildlife. As you glide over the fjords be on the lookout for humpback and killer whales, porpoises, seals, sea lions and the thousands of seabirds (including tufted and horned puffins) that nest on the coast islands. You'll spot bear, Dall sheep and mountain goats on exposed slopes. You'll also fly over the Harding Ice Field, a vast ocean of snow and ice that is the source of some 36 glaciers radiating out in all directions. Your hour-plus trip over the pristine fjords, bays and forests of "Harbor Country" begins and ends at the Seward Airport. **Year Round.**

Harbor Air. PO Box 269, Seward Airport, Seward, AK 99664. (907) 224-3133.

NORTH GULF COAST CHARTER

Operating out of Seward at the head of Resurrection Bay, Mariah Charters visits some of Alaska's most beautiful marine environments. The North Gulf Coast and Kenai Fjords offer unequaled opportunities for close-up viewing and enjoyment of active glaciers, large bird rookeries, (some of the largest concentrations of puffins, murres, and kittiwakes in the north Pacific), and marine mammals, including the always delightful sea otter. Spring and summer bring large numbers of bald eagles, as well as many whales on their annual migration. If you wish to photograph, kayak, fish, or hunt, Mariah offers a range of options including a pickup/dropoff service and charters by the half or full day, overnight or by the week. Charters are limited to five to twenty persons to insure a personalized experience. **April-Oct.**

Mariah Charters. 3812 Katmai Circle, Anchorage, AK 99503. (907) 243-1238.

Arno

KENAI FJORDS BY ZODIAC

Adventure by Zodiac into the remote wilderness of Kenai Fjords, one of the biologically richest habitats in Alaska. Mobile camps, inflatable motorized Zodiacs, and float plane support allow you to explore the most remote areas of the Kenai Fjords in comfort. Far beyond roads and boat harbors you'll enjoy spectacular scenery, photography, and fishing. The only other anglers you're likely to see are sea lions and brown bears. Zodiacs provide an extra margin of safety to take advantage of clear, storm-free days to explore the outer islands for sea lion haul-outs, seabird rookeries or beach combing sites. You can explore protected bays and fjords with ocean kayaks, which are also provided. Trips are limited to six people, with one guide for every two people. **June-Sept.**

Alaska Sojourns. PO Box 87-1410, Wasilla, AK 99687. (907) 376-2913.

SIGHTSEEING/SAILING KENAI FJORDS

Sailing is an exhilarating way to explore the beautifully rugged Kenai Fjords. From your floating observation deck you'll see whales, seals, sea lions, porpoises and sea otter. Numerous sea birds, including the colorful puffin, come within easy camera range. You'll scan beaches for roaming bear, view tidewater glaciers and watch graceful mountain goats climb granite peaks. Anchoring in protected bays, you can go ashore to picnic or explore. The Camai, docked in Seward, is a luxurious 55' Ketch custom built for chartering in Alaska. For your viewing comfort it has an enclosed pilothouse. Private staterooms, showers, dinettes, and a large, safe deck make this trip comfortable and enjoyable for all ages. **June-Aug.**

Camai Yacht Charters. 12800 Saunders Rd., Anchorage, AK 99516. (907) 333-1916.

State Ferry System
Southcentral

The Alaska State Ferry accommodates both vehicles and walk-on passengers and offers a scenic, relaxing and economical way to visit the state's southern coastal regions. The most popular trip in the southcentral system is a seven-hour run between the road-accessible town of Valdez (through Prince William Sound via the Columbia Glacier) and the town of Whittier, which is connected to road systems by a short rail shuttle. Twice a week during the summer, ferries run to the remote fishing town of Cordova on the Copper River Delta from Whittier (7 hours) or Valdez (5 1/2 hours) Once a week, a two-day round trip route connects Seward (also accessible by road) to Valdez and Cordova.

Periodically during the summer ferries make a 10-hour run between Kodiak Island and Seward or Homer (the western most point to which you can travel by road in North America). Just five times during the summer ferries run to Dutch Harbor in the Aleutian Islands from Homer (almost a 6 day round trip) and Kodiak (just under 4 1/2 days round trip). This is probably the most remote regularly scheduled public transportation route in North America and, due to the distances and the inclement weather, is not for every traveler.

State ferries are informal and comfortable with restaurants, bars, lounges, solariums and open decks with chairs. During the summer season, the Prince William Sound routes have U.S. Forest Service staff on board to present narrative talks, films, slide shows and children's activities.

Reservations are required for vehicles, staterooms and, on some routes, for walk-on passengers. However, standbys are taken on a space available basis. Fares are relatively economical (for example, one-way passenger fare from Valdez to Whittier is $50). Children under age 5 travel free; children ages 6 to 11 are half-fare. Senior citizens and handicapped people can also travel free on a space available basis on some routes.

Information: Alaska Marine Highway, PO Box R, Juneau, AK 99811. 1-800-642-0066; Juneau (907) 456-3941; Anchorage (907) 272-7116; Seattle (206) 632-1970.

Humpback whale breaching on ferry route (Olga von Ziegesar photo/ North Gulf Coast Oceanic Society)

Southcentral

Valdez

Valdez (population 2,800) was given its name in 1790 by Spanish naval officers on a spy mission to investigate the extent of Russian territory in America. A century later prospectors enroute to the Fairbanks and the Klondike gold fields built a tent city here. The small community which persisted long after the mines played out was destroyed by the tidal wave which followed the 1964 earthquake. Advice to move the town to higher ground, originally given over 50 years earlier, was finally followed after the earthquake. This new town boomed in the 1970's when it became the terminus and supertanker port for the 800-mile trans-Alaska oil pipeline.

Today, after the heady days of oil wealth extravagance, Valdez remains an energetic and friendly community. A tour of the oil storage and shipping facility provides a captivating perspective on one of the largest privately funded construction projects ($8 billion) ever undertaken. This facility has processed over three billion barrels of oil and continues to handle over one-and-a-half million barrels per day.

Although Valdez averages over 200 inches of precipitation annually, one out of three days is clear or partly clear. In the winter this precipitation makes Valdez Alaska's "snowiest city" with a record of 31 feet. Winters here are very mild and temperatures rarely drop below zero. Nearby Thompson Pass has the nation's heaviest snowfall, receiving up to 81 feet annually. The city proper has more recorded ice climbs (along the ice falls of Keystone Canyon) than the rest of North America combined.

Valdez is 308 miles from Anchorage via the Richardson highway, and the drive from Thompson Pass in the Chugach Mountains through Keystone Canyon to Valdez is one of the most beautiful in the state. Motorists can also stop along the highway in Thompson Pass and hike right to the edge of the Worthington Glacier. Valdez is the most northerly ice-free port in the Northern Hemisphere and is served by the State ferry system. This community is a gateway to Prince William Sound and the surrounding Chugach National Forest. The major attraction in Prince William Sound is the 441 square mile Columbia glacier, a tidewater glacier which forms a blue ice wall forty stories high. The community is also served by scheduled airlines and offers a selection of modern hotels, bed and breakfast inns and campsites.

Information: Valdez Convention and Visitors Bureau. Box 1603-AV, Valdez, AK 99686. (907) 835-2984.

Valdez Arm and trans-Alaska pipeline terminus (VCC photo)

COLUMBIA GLACIER CRUISE

Join a family of year-round Alaskans on a six and a half hour cruise through Prince William Sound to Columbia Glacier aboard the 80 ft. Glacier Spirit, berthed in Valdez. You can watch geologic history in the making as the Columbia Glacier calves and sends giant icebergs floating by. Wildlife enthusiasts and photography buffs will enjoy viewing playful sea otters, seals, sea lions, doll porpoises, whales and hundreds of bird species in their natural habitat. Your cruise will take you around Blyth Island and past the Indian village of Tatitlek with its traditional Russian Orthodox church. You will also visit one of the many inland coves and, in season, watch commercial fishing vessels at work. **May-Sept.**

Stan Stevens Charters. PO Box 1297, Valdez, AK 99686. (907) 835-4731.

ACVB

VALDEZ SALMON/HALIBUT DERBIES

It feels like a 20 pounder on your line...you're already conjuring up visions of how you'll spend that $10,000 first prize. You've found Alaska's secret fishing hole-- Valdez! Each summer the Valdez Chamber of Commerce sponsors monthly fishing derbies beginning in June with the Valdez Halibut Derby. July brings the Valdez Pink Salmon Derby. The entire month of August is set aside for the summer's biggest event--the 35-year-old Valdez Silver Salmon Derby. Renowned for some of the largest silvers in Alaska, Valdez boasts catches of 18-22 lb. fish every year. Six hotels, numerous bed and breakfast inns, two camper parks, free tent camping facilities, and thirteen eateries complement this uncrowded, scenic fishing country. Valdez is truly the place where you can "get away to it all." **June-Aug.**

Valdez Fishing Derbies. Valdez Chamber of Commerce, PO Box 512, Valdez, AK 99686. (907) 835-2330.

FLIGHTSEEING COLUMBIA GLACIER

These Valdez based flightseeing trips offer remarkable views of the rapidly retreating Columbia Glacier. Calving icebergs bigger than a city block break away at the terminus. Harbor seals bask on the numerous icebergs of Columbia Bay. The remains of gold mines are evident along the rocky cliffs near the glacier. Glacier dammed lakes and deep blue pools of water sparkle in the sun. Icefalls cascade thousands of feet on the flanks of Columbia Peak. Mountain goats scamper on the Great Nunatak, a mountain peak surrounded by ice. The Columbia Glacier area and surrounding Chugach Range boast the highest concentration of glaciers in Alaska-- 8,200 square miles of ice. **June-Aug.**

Alpine Aviation. PO Box 1909, Valdez, AK 99686. (907) 835-4304.

PRINCE WILLIAM SOUND EXCURSION

Experience the grandeur of Prince William Sound in luxury aboard the 38' motor yacht "Waterbed," berthed in Whittier. You'll cruise the protected waters of island passages and spend the night in secluded, serene bays where a variety of wildlife, marine mammals and sea birds abound. You'll also enjoy majestic tidewater glaciers at College and Harriman Fjords and watch otters and seals while eagles sweep overhead. There are coves, ocean beaches, mountain lakes, waterfalls, and numerous land glaciers to explore. You can participate in fishing, shrimping, clamming or crabbing to provide the daily seafood entree. This wilderness experience offers the sportsperson, sightseer or naturalist the opportunity to travel in a pleasurable and economical manner. **April-Dec.**

Choice Marine Charters. PO Box 200592, Anchorage, AK 99520-0592. (907) 243-0069.

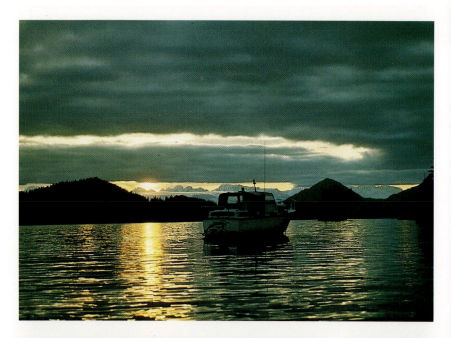

VALDEZ HELICOPTER TOUR

Leave the port of Valdez by helicopter, skimming alongside the 1,000-foot high rock walls of the Keystone Canyon. You will fly over Old Valdez, the original townsite destroyed by the tsunami (tidal wave) which followed the 1964 earthquake. Your aerial vantage point gives you a sweeping perspective of the town that lies at the terminus of the 800-mile trans-Alaska oil pipeline. As you travel back toward Valdez, watch the south side of the harbor for the mountain goats and sheep which populate the Chugach mountains; to the west, enjoy views of the Shoup glacier; and to the northwest, the stunning Valdez glacier. This trip lasts 25 minutes. **Year Round.**

Alaska Wilderness Travel. 121 W. Fireweed, Anchorage, AK 99503. (907) 277-7671, 1-800-544-2236.

SHOUP GLACIER SIGHTSEEING

The Shoup Glacier adventure is an 8-hour trip starting in Valdez. The bay at Shoup Glacier is home to about 100 seals, black bear, mountain goats and a large variety of birds. A black-legged kittiwake rookery here supports some 10,000 birds. The trip allows time to walk up and touch the glacier, look for ice caves and marvel at the delicate beauty of the many wildflowers. You'll also enjoy a hot, hearty beachside lunch. The trip is paced according to the guests' abilities and interests so everyone, young and old, can enjoy it. **June-Sept.**

Alaska Wilderness Travel. 121 W. Fireweed, Anchorage, AK 99503. (907) 277-7671, 1-800-544-2236.

Mark Newman

Mike Thompson

SAILING PRINCE WILLIAM SOUND

Across the rugged Chugach Range just southeast of Anchorage lies one of Alaska's most exciting and spectacular adventure travel destinations -- Prince William Sound. Here, 2,500 miles of pristine coastline await you. And, there is no better way to experience this remarkable area than under sail. Gliding silently with the wind on your 6-day voyage, you'll explore glacially sculpted fjords, emerald conifer-covered islands, and quiet secluded coves. You can visit thundering tidewater glaciers, hike lush meadows and ridges, observe black bear fishing for salmon, watch harbor seals, sea lions, porpoises and whales, and observe nearly 200 species of birds. Experienced sailors can sail a boat themselves. Novices can enjoy the services of your Coast Guard licensed skipper/naturalists. **June-Aug.**

Alaska Wilderness Sailing Safaris. PO Box 1313, Valdez, AK 99686. (907) 835-5175.

GLACIERS OF PRINCE WILLIAM SOUND BY KAYAK

A dozen glaciers overhang the secluded Harriman Fjord, often referred to as "Little Glacier Bay." In your swift, stable touring kayaks you will slip silently among the ice floes to watch harbor seals, sea otters, and birds that bask and play in this habitat. The only sounds you hear are the sounds of nature--the rushing of waterfalls, whirring wings of pigeon guillemots, crackling of ice, and booming of calving glaciers. You'll discover the intrigue of whale watching as you kayak through waters inhabited by humpback and minke whales. Pristine beaches are frequent and hiking opportunities are excellent. Whittier, your starting point, is accessible by train from Anchorage or Portage. From Whittier, a charter boat will transport you 45 miles to the protected waters of Harriman Fjord. **May-Aug.**

Alaska Sea Kayaking. Box 1386, Palmer, AK 99645. (907) 745-3487.

KENNICOTT MOUNTAIN BIKING

Kennicott in Wrangell-St. Elias National Park is the site of a copper mine completed in 1913 by financiers Guggenheim and Morgan at a cost of 23 million dollars and shut down in 1938 after paying 300 million dollars. The wilderness has reclaimed much of the railway running to Kennicott. The mining boom towns are now populated only by a few who stayed or those who came later to enjoy the rugged beauty of this area. The old roads which crisscross this area make for good mountain biking. You'll bike cottonwood and spruce forests, through the old townsite of McCarthy and up to explore the old mine. You'll also bike to the Root Glacier where you'll strap on crampons, rope-up and take a walk on million year old blue ice. Warm, dry beds and home cooked meals await each night. Rafting and flightseeing will complement your week-long adventure here. **June-Aug.**

Alaska Wildwater. Goo Vogt, 7621 Randomar, Anchorage, AK 99507. (907) 344-0035.

Southcentral

Wrangell-St. Elias
National Park and Preserve

The Wrangell-St. Elias National Park and Preserve abuts Canada's Kluane National Park which sits just across the Yukon-Alaska border. Together they have been placed on the internationally recognized World Heritage List for outstanding natural areas. The Wrangell, St. Elias, and Chugach mountain ranges all converge here. The park and preserve contains the continent's greatest collection of peaks over 4,875 meters (16,000 feet) in elevation. Mount St. Elias, at 5,488 meters (18,008 feet), is the second highest peak in the United States (after Mt. McKinley) and the St. Elias mountains are the highest coastal mountains in the world.

The park and preserve encompasses the continent's largest assemblage of glaciers, including the 80-mile long Bagley Ice Field which is the source for the two largest glaciers in North America, the Bering and the Malispina. The Malispina itself is larger than the state of Rhode Island. The park and preserve also contains six major river systems and embraces coastal beaches on the Gulf of Alaska.

The area provides many opportunities for wilderness backpacking, lake fishing, car camping, river running, cross-country skiing, and mountain climbing. In both size and numbers, the Dall sheep populations of the Wrangells are considered the world's finest. At 13.2 million acres, the park and preserve is the nation's largest.

Visitors can reach the park and preserve by road (4-wheel drive or high-clearance vehicles) from Chitina to McCarthy (generally passable in summer), by road from Slana on the Tok cutoff to Nabesna, and by air from Glenallen, Yakutat or Gulkana, which is 322 kilometers (200 miles) by paved highway from Anchorage.

Information: Superintendent, Wrangell-St. Elias National Park and Preserve, PO Box 29, Glenallen, AK 99588. (907) 271-4243.

Climbers ascending west ridge of Mt. Saint Elias (Bob Jacobs photo/ St. Elias Alpine Guides)

Bob Jacobs

FIRST ASCENTS, ST. ELIAS RANGE

Be the first! Climb unnamed peaks in remote and unexplored regions. You can choose routes of various levels of difficulty from hundreds of unclimbed peaks. You'll see no other footprints, no evidence of man in what has been called "North America's Himalayas." Wrangell/St. Elias contains 9 of the 16 highest peaks in North America. Trip leader, Bob Jacobs, a friendly and knowledgeable veteran of the 1985 North Pole Expedition and 15 years of climbing around the world, has led numerous first ascents in this area. Instruction and complete outfitting is available. The length of your trip depends on the peak chosen. Access is generally by ski plane. **May-Sept.**

St. Elias Alpine Guides. PO Box 111241-A, Anchorage, AK 99511. (907) 277-6867.

Bob Jacobs

McCARTHY BED & BREAKFAST, WRANGELL/ST. ELIAS

Discover the Wrangell/St. Elias National Park from the historic village of McCarthy in the heart of the park. The Wrangell/St. Elias has been declared a World Heritage Area by the United Nations as one of the world's last great wilderness areas. Your hosts, Bob and Babbie Jacobs, have lived, taught, and guided in Wrangell/St. Elias for over a decade, taking guests up first ascents on previously unnamed peaks and hiking untold remote valleys to glimpse abundant wildlife including grizzly, Dall sheep, moose, and caribou. Join them for a three-night, four-day adventure which includes a tour of the historic Kennicott mine, a trip on the glacier highways of the park, a short raft trip through the whitewater of the Kennicott River, and the relaxation of a wood-fired sauna. **May-Sept.**

St. Elias Alpine Guides. Box 111241, Anchorage, AK 99511. (907) 277-6867.

COPPER RIVER EXPLORATORY

Your adventure begins with a drive or a flight to the village of McCarthy in the heart of Wrangell-St. Elias Park. Here you'll begin a raft trip following four rivers past sheer-walled canyonlands, glaciers and a Himalaya-like string of unexplored mountains. Along the way you'll see railroad and mining relics from the early 1900's. The Copper River Delta at the end of your float holds one of the world's highest concentrations of bird life. Your guides are versed in the history and geography of the area and are experienced wilderness travellers. In the evenings you'll relax, enjoying sumptuous meals and perhaps music. After taking out near the fishing town of Cordova, you'll enjoy a ferry, rail and car shuttle back to Anchorage. **June-Sept.**

Alaska Wilderness Co-op. 4341 MacAlister Dr., Anchorage, AK 99515. (907) 243-3068.

Chuck Ash photo / Hugh Glass Backpacking Co.

Bear Facts

    The polar bear is the world's largest land carnivore. It lives and hunts on the arctic ice pack. Females come ashore only to have their young. The Alaska brown bear is world's next largest bear. Kodiak Island once held the state's largest browns (l,600 pounds was not an uncommon weight for a large male). As a result of heavier trophy hunting and competing land uses on Kodiak Island, Admiralty Island now boasts Alaska's largest browns and the Alaska Peninsula now has the distinction of having the world's densest brown bear populations. Inland browns, known as grizzlies, are not quite as large (or as well fed) as their coastal cousins. Black bears, the smallest of Alaska's bears, are found throughout the state except the far north and far west.

    Bears originated in and once populated most of northern Asia and Europe. Like humans, bears migrated across the Bering Land Bridge and populated most of North America. Today the populations of Europe and Asia have been decimated. In North America only 50,000 bears remain, mostly in western Canada and Alaska. Only 900 brown bear remain in small pockets (such as Yellowstone) in the continental United States.

    Bear attacks are rare but can occur if a bear is surprised or provoked or if its territory is encroached upon. Sows with cubs, injured bears or bears attracted by food can be especially dangerous. Making lots of noise, walking with the wind when in thick brush, leaving dogs home, sealing and storing food carefully and using a telephoto are all wise practices. Running from a bear is risky unless a safe refuge is very close. Backing away slowly is often safer.

WRANGELL MOUNTAINS TREK

Envision this collage...volcanoes shrouded in an eon of snow, outstretched glacial fingers kneading the earth, blue ice, stone of ochre and rust, and a tundra palette of wildflowers. Trek the high Wrangells where the syrup of geologic change is visible. This is mountain wilderness at its best. The Wrangells are home to Dall sheep, grizzly bear, wolf, wolverine, caribou, and moose. Your feet will follow theirs. You'll traverse from timberline to alpine tundra, cross a mountain pass and descend back to timberline again, all in the shadow of the great peaks of the Wrangells. This fully outfitted adventure originates in Anchorage. Access to the mountains is by road, then bush plane. The trek takes place entirely within the roadless wilderness of Wrangell-St. Elias National Park. Seven and ten-day trips are offered. June-Aug.

**Hugh Glass Backpacking Co.
PO Box 110796-A, Anchorage, AK 99511. (907) 243-1922.**

KLUTINA RIVER RAFTING

The Chugach Mountains provide a backdrop as your floatplane leaves Snowshoe Lake, near Glennallen, and later touches down on Klutina Lake to begin this two-day outing. During the first few miles a professional guide will instruct your group and organize you into an effective paddle crew. You will then descend into the Klutina Gorge, where churning glacial rapids and standing waves provide heart-pounding exhilaration. At day's end a gourmet meal served around the campfire helps replenish exhausted paddlers, and stories of the day's ride are shared. Your trip down the Klutina may include sighting some of the many animals native to the region, including bald eagles, moose, bear, and caribou. **June-Sept.**

Alaska Whitewater. PO Box 142294, Anchorage, AK 99503. (907) 338-0471.

John Fowler

CHISANA WILDERNESS HORSEBACK TRIP

Nestled between the Wrangell Mountains (on the south and west) and the Nutzotin Range (on the north and east) is Chisana, the site of the last big gold rush in Alaska. Still accessible only by air, Chisana is the outfitting point for your horsepack trip. Your well-trained riding horse will carry you along alpine ridges and across wide, open valleys. Dall sheep, caribou, moose, grizzly bear, arctic wolf, wolverine and other game abound in these mountains. Your trip of seven days (or longer) may include sport fishing and gold panning in the lakes and streams, hikes to observe the wildflowers at close range, and photographing the surrounding mountains, glaciers and wildlife. Pack horses will carry everything your guide needs to make comfortable tent camps. Family and group rates available. Best month: **July.**

Alaska Wilderness Travel. 121 W. Fireweed, Anchorage, AK 99503. (907) 277-7671, 1-800-544-2236.

CHICKALOON RIVER HELI-RAFTING

Designed for the wildwater enthusiast, this two-day adventure takes you into the heart of a rarely traveled wilderness in the beautiful Talkeetna Mountains. Your staging point is Chickaloon Station, an hour and a half northeast of Anchorage by road. Here you will board a helicopter for an exciting and spectacular shuttle flight up the Chickaloon. Once there you enjoy lunch on the river before pushing off. That evening you pitch camp at the foot of Castle Mountain. You will have time to hike or just relax around the campfire and experience the timelessness of Alaska's backcountry. Day two begins with a hearty breakfast and an unforgettable river run. Hang on! **June-Aug.**

Alaska Wilderness Travel. 121 W. Fireweed, Anchorage, AK 99503. (907) 277-7671, 1-800-544-2236.

Interior

Interior Alaska is a vast region lying between the Alaska Range and the southern slopes of the Brooks Range. While Denali National Park and Preserve with its massive mountains is certainly the best known and most popular attraction in the Interior, the expansive forested lowlands of its many river systems are much more characteristic of this area.

The Nowitna, Koyukuk, Kanuti, Yukon Flats and Tetlin National Wildlife Refuges, Yukon-Charlie National Preserve, Steese National Conservation Area, and White Mountains National Recreation Area provide millions of acres of prime wildlife habitat. Though these preserves are not heavily visited, hunting, fishing and recreational opportunities in most of them are excellent.

The topography of the Interior consists largely of rolling hills and river lowlands covered by boreal forests of spruce and paper birch. The vegetation in the Interior forms beautiful mosaic patterns illustrating the effects of wildfires, changing river courses, ponding caused by permafrost, and topographical orientation to sunlight. The area has some of the best summer weather in the state with very little rain fall (only about 12 inches of precipitation annually), continuous light and temperatures that climb into the 80's and 90's. This continental climate is also characterized by winter weather which is actually colder than that experienced in much of the Arctic.

Only the central and eastern portions of the Interior are accessible by road. The Fairbanks Borough is the only community of substantial size. The remainder of the region is sparsely populated with small villages, inhabited mostly by Athabascan Indians, scattered along the river systems. The habitat created by these rivers make possible a subsistence livelihood of fishing, hunting and trapping.

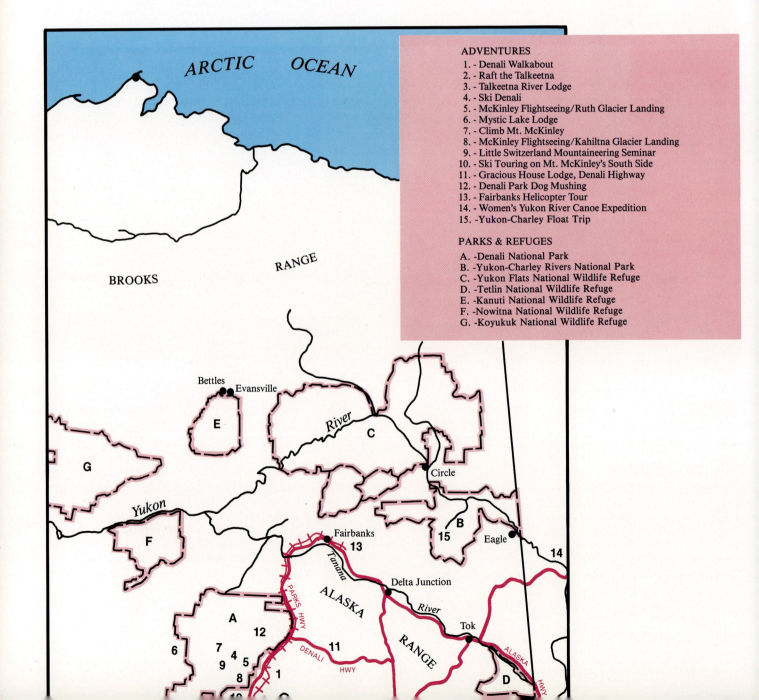

ADVENTURES
1. - Denali Walkabout
2. - Raft the Talkeetna
3. - Talkeetna River Lodge
4. - Ski Denali
5. - McKinley Flightseeing/Ruth Glacier Landing
6. - Mystic Lake Lodge
7. - Climb Mt. McKinley
8. - McKinley Flightseeing/Kahiltna Glacier Landing
9. - Little Switzerland Mountaineering Seminar
10. - Ski Touring on Mt. McKinley's South Side
11. - Gracious House Lodge, Denali Highway
12. - Denali Park Dog Mushing
13. - Fairbanks Helicopter Tour
14. - Women's Yukon River Canoe Expedition
15. - Yukon-Charley Float Trip

PARKS & REFUGES
A. - Denali National Park
B. - Yukon-Charley Rivers National Park
C. - Yukon Flats National Wildlife Refuge
D. - Tetlin National Wildlife Refuge
E. - Kanuti National Wildlife Refuge
F. - Nowitna National Wildlife Refuge
G. - Koyukuk National Wildlife Refuge

Fishing on the Susitna River, beneath Mt. McKinley (John Fowler photo)

Interior

Alaska Railroad
Northbound

This informal, comfortable line running north-south through Southcentral Alaska and into the Interior is an economical and enjoyable way to see some of the state's most dramatic wilderness. Conversation shared with hikers, fishers, homesteaders and other locals who commute via the railroad, make the train itself as much of an adventure as the beautiful views.

The most popular railroad route is the eight-hour trip from Anchorage to Denali National Park. This trip runs through the rich farmlands of the Matanuska Valley and into the vast Susitna River drainage with its boreal forests, speckled with lakes and connecting waterways. Along the way you can enjoy vistas bordered by the Chugach, Chigmit, Talkeetna and Alaska mountain ranges as well as excellent views of Mt. McKinley. If you are a climber, or enjoy getting off the beaten path, you may want to take the local run to Talkeetna, the staging area for Mt. McKinley climbs. The one-day stopover at Denali National Park and Preserve allows you just enough time to take a bus into the park for close-up views of Mt. McKinley, observation of wildlife, and hiking opportunities. After Denali, Fairbanks is the most popular rail destination and the line's northern terminus. The total trip time between Anchorage and Fairbanks is roughly eleven hours.

From mid-May to mid-September an express train runs daily each morning from both Anchorage and Fairbanks. Two days each week a local run makes flag-stops for backpackers and homesteaders. During the winter, schedules vary. Reservations are required.

The railroad also offers several packaged tours which include transportation and lodging. To make the most of rail travel, ask about the railroad's 10-day Unlimited Rail Pass.

Information: Passenger Services, The Alaska Railroad, PO Box 107500, Anchorage, AK 99510. (907) 265-2494 (Anchorage); (907) 456-4155 (Fairbanks).

Alaska Railroad northbound (ACVB photo)

John Fowler

DENALI WALKABOUT

Two long ridges rising between the Susitna and Chulitna rivers command a sweeping view of 20,300-foot Mt. McKinley and a host of snow-covered neighboring peaks and glaciers. Indian and Curry ridges form a 30-mile-long alpine tundra plateau, pocketed with lakes, tarns, and fascinating rock formations. This backpack trip, with trailhead access along the Parks Highway midway between Anchorage and Fairbanks, takes you above the timberline alongside ice-scoured and wind-sculpted geological formations and colorful tundra plant communities. Footing will range from striding along a carpet of lichens, heather, or pebbled outcrops to scrambling over boulders or slogging through wet grass and bogs. Alpine flowers appear where snow has recently melted. Wild berries are common in August. Pack dogs will help carry gear on this 10-day outing. **June-Sept.**

Alaska Wilderness Travel. 121 W. Fireweed, Anchorage, AK 99503. (907) 277-7671, 1-800-544-2236.

RAFT THE TALKEETNA RIVER

With 18 miles of challenging class III-V whitewater, excellent fishing, and abundant wildlife, including grizzly bear and bald eagles, the Talkeetna is one of the most exciting and scenic river trips in Alaska. Starting in the historic town of Talkeetna, a bush plane will fly you into the heart of the Talkeetna Range. Because of the challenging whitewater, this area remains pristine and relatively untraveled. The first day of this 3-5 day trip you will enjoy a leisurely float with plenty of time for fishing. Day two brings you to the "Entrance Exam." Then hang on for a roller coaster ride through the Talkeetna canyon! Your trip will end as leisurely as it began as you float through more good fishing country and into the town of Talkeetna. Nova Riverrunners has over 21 years experience in Alaska's backcountry. **June-Sept.**

Nova Riverrunners. SRC Box 8337/Chickaloon, Palmer, AK 99645. (907) 745-5753.

TALKEETNA RIVER LODGE

The Talkeetna, a Tanaina Indian word for "river of plenty," is part of the Susitna River drainage system which boasts the second largest run of migrating fish in the world. Your lodge is situated at the confluence of the Talkeetna River and Chunilna Creek. From here, comfortable Jetline riverboats and experienced guides give you access to over 200 miles of prime fishing territory. You can fish for all five species of salmon as well as trout, dolly varden and grayling. Five spacious cedar cabins provide lodging for up to 20 guests. Hearty Alaskan style meals are served in the main lodge. After dinner you can enjoy a relaxing sauna or settle back on one of the sun decks overlooking the river. **June-Aug.**

Alaska Wilderness Travel. 121 W. Fireweed, Anchorage, AK 99503. (907) 277-7671, 1-800-544-2236.

Interior

Denali
National Park and Preserve

Mount McKinley, at 6,105 meters (20,320 feet), is North America's highest mountain. Measured from base to summit it is the world's highest mountain, overshadowing Mt. Everest by some 2,000 to 3,000 feet of vertical rise. The Athabascan Indians called it Denali, "The High One," and in 1980 the park's name was changed to Denali.

The Denali Fault, a significant formative feature of the Alaska Range and the largest crustal break in North America, arcs 600 miles across the center of Alaska. Under the shadow of the range, visitors can observe unusually concentrated and accessible populations of barren-ground caribou, grizzly bear, wolves, moose, Dall sheep, and other wildlife. Meandering, glacier-born rivers laden with silt (or rock flour) create natural dams and periodically change course across the wide, flat northern valleys. The park and preserve encompass some 6 million acres.

Denali is accessible by car, railroad, motorcoach and scheduled air service. Shuttle bus service operates within the park itself along the 138-kilometer (85-mile) wilderness road from the entrance to Wonder Lake. The shuttle bus will drop you off or pick you up wherever you like at no cost. Unlike many of Alaska's parklands, a variety of lodging and facilities are located in and near the park.

Information: Superintendent, Denali National Park and Preserve, PO Box 9, McKinley Park, AK 99755. (907) 271-4243.

*Mt. McKinley
from alpine meadow
(DOT photo)*

Genet Expeditions

SKI DENALI

Enjoy spring skiing in one of the world's most spectacular mountain/glacier areas, just a half-hour's flight from Talkeetna. You'll ski-tour across the vast Sheldon Amphitheater and into the Great Gorge of the Ruth Glacier. Nearby slopes offer downhill skiing suited to every ability--all with magnificent views of Mt. McKinley, Silverthrone, the Moose's Tooth, and a host of other snow-clad peaks. The Don Sheldon Mountain House will be your cozy base with its wood stove and accommodations for up to six people. Those who spend the night will fall asleep to the faint rumble of distant avalanches. Photographic opportunities are unlimited, and guided ski tours are available. Lowell Thomas, Jr., owner and chief pilot of Talkeetna Air Taxi, has been flying this and other McKinley areas for over twenty years. **March-Aug.**

Talkeetna Air Taxi. PO Box 73, Talkeetna, AK 99676. (907) 733-2218.

McKINLEY FLIGHTSEEING AND RUTH GLACIER LANDING

Explore Denali National Park by air and experience McKinley close up with K2 Aviation glacier pilots. Taking off from historic Talkeetna, the immense scale of Alaska unfolds around you. The broad, forested Susitna River Valley gives way to the towering peaks of the Alaska Range. You'll fly over sculptured ridges and immense, glacier-filled valleys to the towering walls of McKinley, so close that the magnificent mountain fills half the horizon. Experience the excitement of a glacier landing and enjoy a spectacular view of Denali from the Don Sheldon Amphitheater, a vast expanse of gleaming ice and snow surrounded by towering peaks. The return flight follows the Ruth Glacier's course for 25 miles through the Great Gorge and into the forested Chulitna valley. **April-Sept.** Flightseeing available year round.

K2 Aviation. Box 290A, Talkeetna, AK 99676. (907) 733-2291.

George Palmer

MYSTIC LAKE LODGE

Located on the north slope of the Alaska Range adjacent to Denali National Park lies Mystic Lake, 50 miles to the west and in full view of Mt. McKinley. Accessible only by aircraft, this remote lodge offers guided wildlife photo safaris, Alaska Range backpacking, big game hunts, and custom sportfishing. Fish one day on Mystic Lake for lake trout and northern pike; then fly with your pilot/guide 300 miles to the rain forests of Prince William Sound where chum, coho, pink, and sockeye salmon, cutthroat trout and dolly varden await your offering. Excellent rainbow trout, grayling, and king salmon fishing are available within a 30 minute flight of the lodge. **May-Oct.**

Mystic Lake Lodge. George Palmer, Box 887, Palmer, AK 99645. (907) 745-3168.

Galen Rowell

CLIMB MT. McKINLEY

Genet Expeditions has been leading climbing expeditions on Mt. McKinley since 1968. More than 900 climbers have joined them over the past 18 years with well over 75% reaching the summit. Their success rate is due largely to their experienced staff of guides and assistants and to the fact that they have been guiding climbs on McKinley and other great Alaskan peaks longer than any other guide service. Mt. McKinley is North America's highest peak at 20,320 feet. Genet's West Buttress expeditions ascend what has become the classic route up this spectacular mountain. The climb, though not technically difficult, involves six to eight camps along the route. Members will experience high altitude climbing, changeable mountain weather, and some of the most extraordinary scenery in the world. **April-Aug.**

Genet Expeditions. Talkeetna, AK 99676. (907) 376-5120.

MT. McKINLEY FLIGHTSEEING/ KAHILTNA GLACIER LANDING

High among the vast sculptures of rock, snow and ice of the Alaska Range are sights that will astound even the most worldly traveler. Your ski-equipped bush plane will land you on the 7,000 foot level of the Kahiltna Glacier, where you can experience the raw beauty of North America's largest mountains. You will smell the cleanest, purest air and have occasion to talk with sunburned mountain climbers who are attempting the 20,320-foot summit of Denali, "The Great One." All aircrafts are intercom-equipped for your comfort. Owner/operator Doug Geeting has over 11,000 hours total flying time--9,000 of these hours are mountain time. Glacier landings are possible between early April and mid-July. Scenic flights are available year round. **April-July.**

Doug Geeting Aviation. PO Box 42, Talkeetna, AK 99676. (907) 733-2366.

LITTLE SWITZERLAND MOUNTAINEERING SEMINAR

Little Switzerland is located about sixteen miles south of Denali, and offers a variety of climbing adventures and spectacular scenery. The seminar covers basic mountaineering, snow and ice climbing, rock climbing, glacier travel and rescue, avalanche awareness and rescue, and more. It's an "everything you ever wanted to know about climbing, but were afraid to ask" type of experience. The glaciers and mountains around Little Switzerland also offer superb skiing. The seminar runs 7-14 days and is limited to 6-12 climbers. Mountain Trip has taught climbing in this area since 1973 and has an excellent reputation. Ask climbers about them! Then join Mountain Trip for a fun and rewarding experience in the mountains of the Alaska Range. **June-July.**

Mountain Trip. Gary Bocarde, Box 91161, Anchorage, AK 99509. (907) 345-6499.

SKI TOURING ON MT. McKINLEY'S SOUTH SIDE

Thirty-five miles from the summit of Mt. McKinley lie the boreal forest, muskeg, tundra, and river lowland of the Swan Lake and Tokositna River region. Here you can cross-country ski across trackless snow, exploring the southeast border of Denali National Park where massive glaciers of the Alaska Range meet the forest. You'll enjoy striking wilderness panoramas as spring begins. Animals are moving around, and the snow is at its best for touring or telemarking. The northern lights add color to the night sky. You'll experience the unique lifestyle of living in a remote, family-built, log cabin at the foot of the Alaska Range. This seven-day trip, led by Swan Lake residents, departs from Anchorage. It is designed for 6-8 intermediate cross-country skiers enthusiastic about backcountry ski touring. **Feb-May.**

Alaska-Denali Guiding, Inc. Brian and Diane Okonek, Box 326, Talkeetna, AK 99676. (907) 733-2649.

GRACIOUS HOUSE LODGE, DENALI HIGHWAY

Located beside the Susitna River, a short drive from Mt. McKinley/Denali National Park, Gracious House Lodge is an old and respected country-style lodge. Operators and 30-year residents Butch and Carol Gratias are known for their hospitality and knowledge of the area. Gracious House offers home-cooking on a vintage woodstove and grill, excellent lake trout and grayling fishing, horseback trips, photography, goldpanning, abundant wildlife and fantastic scenery. Relax in Gracious House's comfortable cocktail lounge,"The Sluice Box Bar," with its goldmining atmosphere. Charter air services offer quick, convenient access to remote lakes and glacier flightseeing. Modern cabins and bunkhouse accommodations are available. **June-Sept.**

Gracious House Lodge & Flying Service. 859 Elaine Dr., Anchorage, AK 99504. (907) 333-3148.

DENALI PARK DOG MUSHING

Many backcountry Alaskans feel that winter is the best time to visit Alaska. Winter brings exquisite colors and a marvelous solitude to the outdoors. The days are crisp and clear and the evening skies are filled with millions of stars and sporadic displays of shimmering Northern Lights. On this 3-day dog mushing tour in Denali National Park you'll take turns riding the dog sled and driving your own team through a true winter wonderland. Your trail leads to the foot of the Ruth Glacier where you are likely to spot moose and perhaps wolves. You'll spend your evenings in a warm, cozy cabin. Pack your Jack London and come experience the call of the wild. **Sept-May.**

Alaska Wilderness Travel. 121 W. Fireweed, Anchorage, AK 99503. (907) 277-7671, 1-800-544-2236.

Fairbanks

Fairbanks Borough (population 59,000) is a service and commercial center for Interior Alaska, a supply point for the trans-Alaska pipeline, and a jumping-off point for trips into the Interior and the Arctic. The borough is often a first "port of call" for motorists arriving in the State from Canada. Road systems radiate out from Fairbanks to Manley Hot Springs, Dietrich Camp, Circle, Eagle, Tok and Denali National Park. Scheduled and chartered air service is available from Fairbanks to outlying villages, and travel is also possible on the Nenana, Tanana, and Yukon rivers after the ice goes out in May. Anchorage is 50 minutes away by air, a six-hour drive via the George Parks highway, or an eleven-hour trip by the Alaska Railroad.

Fairbanks began as a gold rush town at the turn of the century. Today Fairbanks is a friendly, energetic town with a "make-do" architectural mix. Weathered buildings and cabins pre-dating the influx of pipeline money are interspersed with more expensive homes and hotels, shopping malls and a university. Alaskaland, a forty-acre theme park with replicas of gold rush cabins and an Eskimo village, is the city's principle tourist attraction.

The continental climate here can go from extremes of 100 degrees in the summer to 60 below in the winter. While Fairbanks has some of the coldest winter weather in the state, spring and summer here are ideal. During the summer, Fairbanks enjoys long daylight hours--in excess of 20 hours a day. In fact, there is enough light for pilots to navigate visually 24 hours a day between April 26 and August 18.

Information: Fairbanks Convention and Visitors Bureau. 550 First Avenue, Fairbanks, AK 99701. (907) 456-5774.

Dogsled racing, popular in the Interior (John Fowler photo)

FAIRBANKS HELICOPTER TOUR

Fairbanks, known as the gateway to Alaska's Interior, is the starting point for your 25-minute helicopter ride. Aerial views of the trans-Alaska oil pipeline will give you a new perspective of this 800-mile engineering feat. You'll examine the Murphy, Esther and Pedro mountain domes for the many gold mines and dredge sites of the gold rush of the late 1800's, some of which are still in operation today. From your lofty vantage point you may well spot bull moose or magnificent bald eagles. You will pass over several rivers, some dotted with sternwheelers. You'll traverse the placid Tanana River, survey the city and its surrounding areas, and travel back to your heli-port by way of the Chena slough. **Year Round.**

Alaska Wilderness Travel. 121 W. Fireweed, Anchorage, AK 99503. (907) 277-7671, 1-800-544-2236.

John Fowler

Aurora Borealis

The Aurora Borealis or Northern Lights ripple and flood across the nighttime sky when electromagnetic forces produced by the resistance of earth's magnetic field (the magnetosphere) to the flow of charged particles from the sun (the solar wind) become a galactic cannon firing huge balls of hot plasma into space. In equilibrium the earth's magnetic field is stretched downwind into a long tail (the magnetotail) over 1,000 times the earth's radius in length. The magnetotail acts like a giant ray gun collecting and energizing solar-wind particles into a hot plasma and shooting the plasma into space at speeds of millions of kilometers per hour. When the magnetotail collects too much plasma (for reasons apparently related to sun spot activity), its field lines are stretched and reform around a giant ball of plasma (a plasmoid) 70 to 80 earth radii long, 20 to 25 earth radii wide and 10 to 12 earth radii high. The plasmoid then fires into space at some 500 to 1,000 kilometers per second.

The collapse in the field lines during the formation of the plasmoid sends electrons showering into the earth's upper atmosphere creating waves of molecular sparks which make up the auroras. Electrons continue to bombard the atmosphere for an additional 30 minutes to two hours while plasma refills the magnetotail stretching it back to its state of equilibrium. Most auroras appear from earth as greenish-white ribbons or curtain shapes fluttering and billowing across the sky. Less frequently auroras may be blue, purple and red and can arch over the heavens like a vaulted dome.

Interior

Yukon-Charley Rivers
National Preserve

The Yukon-Charley Rivers National Preserve contains 185 kilometers (115 miles) of the historic Yukon River and the entire 142-kilometer (88-mile) Charley River basin. Old cabins and relics along the Yukon remain today as evidence of its importance as a transportation route during the Gold Rush era. Archeological and paleontological sites in the preserve provide important information about a much more ancient human and geological past. Today, the Yukon is still an important link between the Athabascan Indian villages along its banks.

The broad and swift Yukon is heavy with silt while, in contrast, the smaller Charley flows crystal clear. The Charley is considered one of Alaska's finest recreational streams. The rivers merge between the gold rush boom towns of Eagle and Circle. Cliffs and bluffs along the two rivers provide nesting habitat for peregrine and gyrfalcons. Navigating the Yukon by raft, canoe, or powerboat, is a popular way to see wildlife and scenery. The Charley River demands more advanced river skills. The 2.2 million acres of the preserve are frequented by grizzly bear, Dall sheep and moose.

Visitors can reach the preserve by way of the Taylor Highway to Eagle or via the Steese Highway from Fairbanks to Circle. Scheduled flights serve both towns from Fairbanks.

Information: Superintendent, Yukon-Charley Rivers National Preserve, PO Box 64, Eagle, AK 99738. (907) 271-4243.

Dusk on the Yukon (Rachael Holzworth-Parker photo/Women of the Wilderness)

John Fowler

WOMEN'S YUKON RIVER CANOE EXPEDITION

The Yukon is the third largest and fifth longest river in the U.S. This three-week, 460-mile expedition will take you from Whitehorse to Dawson past relics of Klondike history, Indian graveyards, sternwheelers, abandoned townsites, snow-covered peaks, open meadows and dense forests. Canoeing this wide, flat, swift-moving river will allow you to get close to beaver, fox, moose, falcons, bald eagles and many other birds. The pace of the expedition allows time for exploring, relaxing and taking in the local color of towns along the way. This expedition is designed for the novice and experienced canoeist alike and provides a safe, supportive, non-competitive approach to learning wilderness skills. **June-Sept.**

Alaska Wilderness Travel. 121 W. Fireweed, Anchorage, AK 99503. (907) 277-7671, 1-800-544-2236.

YUKON-CHARLEY RAFTING

The clear waters of the Charley River, part of the National Wild and Scenic River system, tumble down from an unusually pristine mountain region in the eastern Interior. Home to endangered peregrine falcon as well as gyrfalcon, Dall sheep, and caribou, this drainage has escaped modern incursions because of its class III whitewater and its difficult and remote access. On your sixty mile float down the Charley, you will enjoy watching for wildlife, viewing permafrost along the lower bluffs, fishing for grayling, pike, and sheefish, hiking the backcountry, and running rapids. Weather in this area is often hot and sunny. Upon reaching the historic Yukon, you will learn how to row the raft yourself and assist your guides in travelling this ancient transportation corridor. Takeout is at Circle, a colorful gold rush town which once boasted an opera house and was touted as the "Paris of the North." **June-Aug.**

Alaska Wilderness Co-op. 4341 MacAlister Dr., Anchorage, AK 99515. (907) 243-3068.

John Fowler

Birding In Alaska

Some 405 bird species (half of the total number occuring in the entire continental U.S.) are known to occur in Alaska. Birds from five continents migrate here. In addition, many species also observed outside Alaska are genetically differentiated here or exhibit distinct plumage or behavior in this northern habitat. The state supports the only existing North American populations of 24 species. Each summer, more seabirds inhabit Alaskan waters than exist in the entire continental U.S. Eagles, trumpeter swans, snow geese, sandhill cranes, puffins and many other widely admired species congregate here. Alaska is also home to four endangered species: the American and arctic peregrine falcons, the Aleutian Canada goose, the nearly extinct short-tailed albatross and the Eskimo curlew (now probably extinct). An observant bird watcher here has an excellent chance of documenting new and valuable information.

Interior

Yukon Flats
National Wildlife Refuge

At its northernmost point, the Yukon River spreads unconfined for 200 miles through a vast flood plain protected within the Yukon Flats Refuge. In the spring millions of migrating birds converge on the flats before ice moves from the river. The birds come from four continents to feed on the abundant aquatic food and raise their young. The refuge has one of the highest nesting densities of waterfowl in North America. The 50,000 canvasbacks which nest here constitute 15 percent of the continent's breeding population and represent an important contribution to the continued survival of this species.

Yukon king and chum salmon are among the finest strains in Alaska due to large stores of fat that serve as fuel for their 1,000-2,000 mile spawning journeys, the longest salmon runs in the world. Mammals on the refuge include moose, caribou, Dall sheep, wolves, lynx, and black and grizzly bear. Historically, the Flats have been important for furbearers. Hudson's Bay fur trappers discovered the Flats in the 1830's and established Ft. Yukon, Alaska's oldest English-speaking settlement. Coyotes, once common, have declined in recent years.

Summer temperatures on the Flats are higher than any other place of comparable latitude in North America. It is the only place in the world where temperatures of 100°F have been recorded above the Arctic Circle. The same encircling mountains that make high summer temperatures possible also create a natural frost pocket which make winter temperatures some of the coldest anywhere.

Several rivers here can be floated by canoe, kayak and raft. Fishing for northern pike can be excellent. The clear waters of Birch and Beaver Creeks make them prime canoe streams, possibly Alaska's best. They offer outstanding grayling fishing and along their banks are fossil outcrops and warm water springs. A kayak trip down the Sheenjek River provides an unrivaled wilderness experience.

Information: Refuge Manager, Yukon Flats National Wildlife Refuge, Federal Building and Courthouse, Box 20, 101-12th Avenue, Fairbanks, AK 99701. (907) 456-0440.

Moose habitat on the Porcupine River (M. LeFever photo/FWS)

Tetlin
National Wildlife Refuge

Tetlin is a showcase of the geographic and ecological effects of wildfires, permafrost and fluctuating river channels. The prominent feature on the refuge is an undulating plain interspersed with hills, forests, ponds, lakes and extensive marshes. The Chisana and Nabesna rivers, born from the melting glaciers of the Wrangell Mountains, meander through these wetlands before joining to form the Tanana River. The southern portion of the refuge includes the spruce-covered foothills of the Nutzotin Mountains.

The vegetation of Tetlin is an excellent example of the positive benefits of natural wildfires. When fire destroys a portion of a spruce forest, a series of habitats follow until, once again, spruce forests become dominant. The varied habitats indirectly created by fires allow a diverse group of animals to exist, including a dense moose population, black bear, grizzly bear, ptarmigan, wolf, wolverine, coyote, lynx and red fox. Dall sheep are common in the southwest part of the refuge in the Mentasta Mountains. The lower slopes and foothills provide important winter range for the Chisana caribou herd.

Waterfowl, in breeding concentrations nearly rivaling the famed Yukon Flats, make Tetlin unique among Alaska's interior refuges. Species akin to the Canadian Peace River biotic community breed no farther north than the Tetlin marshes. In some years duck nesting densities go as high as 600 birds per square mile. Tetlin boasts Alaska's greatest concentrations of nesting osprey, and during their fall migration 300,000 sandhill cranes will pause to feed on the wetlands' rich aquatic food.

Hunting and fishing are common activities in the refuge. Moose and waterfowl hunting are especially popular. Major fish species include lake trout, northern pike, grayling and burbot (freshwater lingcod). Salmon and whitefish are common in the Tanana and scientists have discovered a unique population of trout in the upper Tanana drainage that seems to be a genetically isolated strain of dolly varden. Tetlin is accessible from locations along the Alaska Highway.

Information: Refuge Manager, Tetlin National Wildlife Refuge, PO Box 155, Tok, AK 99780. (907) 883-5312.

Tetlin countryside near the Canadian border (FWS photo)

Kanuti
National Wildlife Refuge

The Kanuti refuge straddles the Arctic Circle approximately 150 miles northwest of Fairbanks. This pristine refuge is unique because it preserves an entire solar basin ecosystem of wetlands, treeless tundra uplands and river drainages which surround the Kanuti and Koyukuk rivers.

The refuge provides nesting habitat for waterfowl--primarily Canada and white-fronted geese and a variety of ducks including pintail, American wigeon, scaup, and scoter. During fall migration flights, over 100,000 birds pass through the refuge. Kanuti's contribution as a waterfowl habitat increases when the prairies of south-central Canada and the northern midwestern United States lie baked and dry. Birds displaced from these breeding areas fly northward to escape the drought.

The refuge supports nineteen species of fish including whitefish, northern pike, grayling and salmon. The drainages of the Koyukuk and Kanuti rivers contain vast stands of willow that support a large moose population. The refuge is also home to the Ray Mountain caribou herd--a non-migratory herd that never leaves the region. Other wildlife includes black bear, grizzly bear, wolf and wolverine.

Scenic features of the refuge include Lower Kanuti Canyon, the crags and pinnacles of the Ray Mountains, and the singular geology of Sithylemenkat Lake, formed by an ancient meteor impact. Float trips on the Kanuti and Koyukuk rivers and tributary streams provide a good way to see the refuge. Few people visit Kanuti and those who do primarily hunt, fish and view wildlife. Fishing for northern pike and grayling is excellent. The town of Bettles is the jumping-off point for exploration of the refuge.

Information: Refuge Manager, Kanuti National Wildlife Refuge, Federal Building and Courthouse, Box 20, 101-12th Avenue, Fairbanks, AK 99701. (907) 456-0329.

Canada Geese and brood (John Fowler photo)

Photos by: (top) Sue Miskill; (middle) John Fowler; (bottom) Jon Robbins.

Interior

Nowitna
National Wildlife Refuge

Nowitna consists of forested lowlands, hills, lakes, marshes, ponds, and streams in the central Yukon River Valley. Three quarters of the refuge is wetlands holding over 3,500 lakes and 1,800 miles of rivers and streams. The dominant feature on Nowitna is the Nowitna River--part of the National Wild and Scenic River System. This magnificent river provides crucial spawning grounds for northern pike, sheefish and three species of whitefish. The refuge was established primarily to protect waterfowl habitat. Mallards, American wigeon, pintail and scaup nest here in numbers rivaled only by the Yukon Flats. Nowitna is also a vital nesting area for whistling swans.

Nowitna is one of four refuges--Nowitna, Innoko, Kanuti, and Koyukuk--encompassed by a solar basin. A solar basin is characterized by encircling hills, light winds, low rainfall, very cold winters and short warm summers. The summer sun circles over these refuges without setting.

The refuge's mix of habitats supports varied wildlife. Great numbers of moose and black bear inhabit the lowlands and wooded river courses. Grizzly bear and small clusters of caribou live in the foothills. A variable wolf population fluctuates according to the number of moose and wintering caribou. Furbearers provide income and food for local residents.

The Nowitna River offers a gentle and scenic float. A good trip would begin with a flight to the headwaters of the Nowitna and a float through the Nowitna Canyon. One can continue all the way to the Yukon, taking out at Ruby. Another good trip would start with a drive south from Ruby to the Sulatna River headwaters. One could then float the Sulatna to the Nowitna and the Nowitna to the Yukon, taking out at Ruby. Moose and bear hunting are major activities here. Fishing for northern pike, sheefish and grayling is excellent. The rockhound can go agate collecting or look for ancient outcroppings of fossils on the Upper Nowitna.

Information: Refuge Manager, Nowitna National Wildlife Refuge, PO Box 270, Kotzebue, AK 99752. (907) 442-3799.

Young bull moose browsing (FWS photo)

Koyukuk
National Wildlife Refuge

The Koyukuk flats are an extensive floodplain of the Koyukuk River. The oxbows, sloughs, 15,000 lakes, and some 3,000 miles of rivers and creeks provide habitat for salmon, beaver and waterfowl. These lowlands are surrounded by hills covered with boreal forest. The refuge includes the Nogahabara Dunes--a 10,000 acre active dune field formed about 10,000 years ago from wind-blown deposits. The field is geologically related to the Kobuk Dunes to the north, the only other active dune field in Alaska.

When the spring floodwaters of the Koyukuk River withdraw, gumbo mudflats remain, on which luxuriant mats of new grass quickly grow. This excellent forage attracts nearly 75,000 white-fronted and lesser Canada geese. Some 165 pair of trumpeter swans nest at Koyukuk. In addition, 140,000 ducks feed here on the nutritious pond vegetation of the refuge's shallow lakes. In all, 140 species have been sighted on the refuge. By September more than 400,000 ducks and geese have passed through the refuge to southern wintering grounds.

Black bear are abundant in forest lowlands and grizzly bear inhabit the open tundra. A variety of furbearers are also found here. Trappers from the Koyukuk and Innoko basins supply forty percent of Alaska's beaver catch. Wolves and moose are common. Caribou from the Western Arctic herd often winter on portions of the refuge. King, chum and silver salmon, cisco, arctic grayling, northern pike and whitefish fill the streams and rivers.

Koyukuk has excellent moose hunting and fishing. Trip possibilities include observing nesting waterfowl, exploring the Nogahabara Dunes or watching wildlife while floating the slow moving Koyukuk. A river trip could begin at the town of Hughes and take out at Huslia or begin at Huslia and end at any of the native settlements downstream. Galena is the closest major town to the refuge and it has scheduled air service from Fairbanks.

Information: Refuge Manager, Koyukuk National Wildlife Refuge, PO Box 287, Galena, AK 99741. (907) 656-1231.

Nogahabara Sand Dunes just south of the Arctic Circle (Joe Keller photo/ FWS)

Arctic

The Arctic Circle is the southern boundary of a region encompassing both the southern and northern drainages of the Brooks Range as well as the North Slope, a broad coastal plain running from the Brooks to the edge of the Arctic Ocean. The area is most widely known as the home of the northern, or Inupiaq, Eskimo who live along the coast and hunt migrating whale. More recently the North Slope has also become known for the rich oil fields located at Prudhoe Bay and nearby Kuparuk and for the 800 mile pipeline through which the oil flows south.

During the short summer the North Slope explodes with life. Although this area has desert-like precipitation, low evaporation and an underlying base of permafrost combine with continuous summer sunlight to create vast marshes speckled with thousands of ponds and lakes. These same conditions blanket slopes with delicate green tundra. Hundreds of thousands of birds summer in these wetlands. Free-roaming herds of caribou, musk-ox and Dall sheep, as well as wolves, wolverine and grizzly bear, forage on the tundra. Polar bear live along the coast.

The southern drainage of the Brooks Range is covered with the same boreal forests which typify the Interior. This area also shares the Interior's continental climate with warm, dry summer weather. During the summer, large dune fields found in this region can take on all the characteristics of an equatorial desert. Hundreds of thousands of waterfowl migrate to wetlands here. Caribou, moose, bear and a variety of furbearers are also abundant.

Most of the Arctic is accessible only by air. The Dalton Highway runs north from Fairbanks to Prudhoe Bay but has traditionally been open to the public only as far as Dietrich Camp in the Brooks Range. Bus tours to Prudhoe Bay have recently become available.

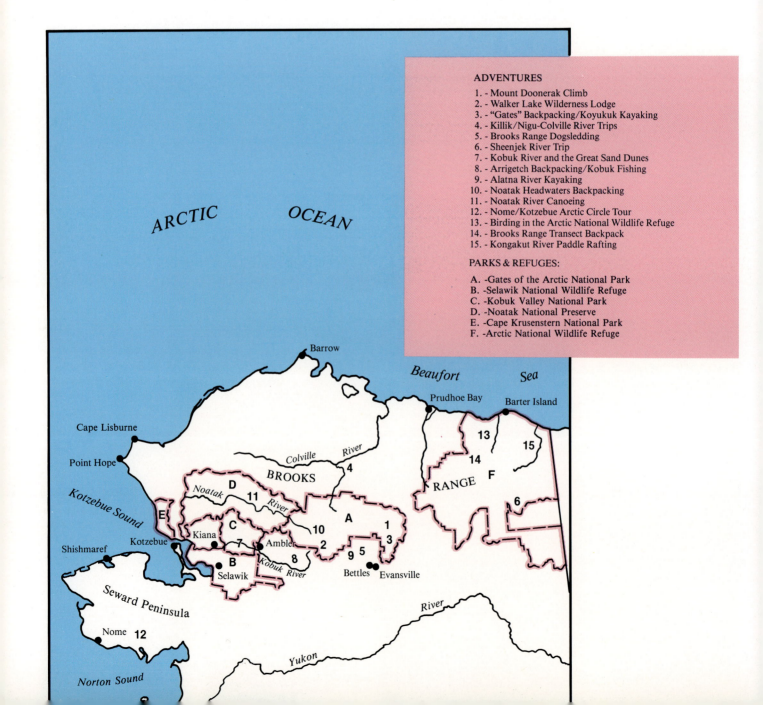

ADVENTURES

1. - Mount Doonerak Climb
2. - Walker Lake Wilderness Lodge
3. - "Gates" Backpacking/Koyukuk Kayaking
4. - Killik/Nigu-Colville River Trips
5. - Brooks Range Dogsledding
6. - Sheenjek River Trip
7. - Kobuk River and the Great Sand Dunes
8. - Arrigetch Backpacking/Kobuk Fishing
9. - Alatna River Kayaking
10. - Noatak Headwaters Backpacking
11. - Noatak River Canoeing
12. - Nome/Kotzebue Arctic Circle Tour
13. - Birding in the Arctic National Wildlife Refuge
14. - Brooks Range Transect Backpack
15. - Kongakut River Paddle Rafting

PARKS & REFUGES:

A. -Gates of the Arctic National Park
B. -Selawik National Wildlife Refuge
C. -Kobuk Valley National Park
D. -Noatak National Preserve
E. -Cape Krusenstern National Park
F. -Arctic National Wildlife Refuge

Arrigetch Peaks in the summer (Gary Goodson photo/Sourdough Outfitters)

Gates of the Arctic
National Park and Preserve

Gates of the Arctic is the exquisite, fragile, and remote wilderness that captured the heart and imagination of arctic explorer Robert Marshall in the 1930's. The park and preserve lies entirely north of the Arctic Circle. During the summer the weather can be as capricious as it is spectacular, prone to snowstorms as well as temperatures approaching 90° F. "The Gates" straddles the crest of the Brooks Range, the northernmost extension of the Rocky Mountains. It forms the headwaters for the Koyukuk, Tinayguk, John, Alatna, Kobuk, and Noatak rivers, all part of the National Wild and Scenic River System. Its southern drainage circumscribes portions of the boreal forest of Alaska's interior and its north slope takes in the edge of the polar desert.

Barren-ground caribou and grizzly bear forage on the vast but fragile Arctic tundra. Two distinct Native cultures live here: the Athabascan Indians of the southern spruce-taiga forests, and the Nunamiut Eskimos, who hunt caribou in the high valleys. Both cultures continue to follow subsistence patterns of life within the eight million acres of the park and preserve.

Scheduled airlines from Fairbanks serve Bettles-Evansville and Anaktuvuk Pass. Charter flights into the park are available from these villages. The Dalton Highway roughly parallels the edge of the park at a distance of 5 to 15 miles.

Information: Superintendent, Gates of the Arctic National Park and Preserve, PO Box 74680, Fairbanks, AK 99707. (907) 271-4243.

The Western Arctic caribou summer migration (FWS photo)

Gary Goodson

MT. DOONERAK CLIMB

Mt. Doonerak, at 7,457 feet, is the tallest peak in a remote area of the central Brooks Range. It has been described as the "Matterhorn of the Arctic" because of its striking likeness to that famous European peak. The name means "spirit" in Eskimo. Mt. Doonerak has been climbed less than ten times. Yours may be the first climb by a guided party. From the summit a panoramic view of hundreds of Brooks Range peaks awaits, including Boreal Mountain and Frigid Crags -- the "Gates of the Arctic." Time and conditions permitting, you'll also climb nearby peaks and have plenty of opportunity for viewing wildlife and scenery. Safety and personal enjoyment will be stressed, with experienced guides leading difficult pitches. Good physical condition is required. Previous climbing experience is helpful, though not required. **June-July.**

Alaska Wilderness Travel. 121 W. Fireweed, Anchorage, AK 99503. (907) 277-7671, 1-800-544-2236.

WALKER LAKE WILDERNESS LODGE

Eighty miles above the Arctic Circle, in an area accessible only by air, is the Walker Lake Wilderness Lodge-- the only lodge within the vast Gates of the Arctic National Park. In April you can cross-country ski beneath brilliant blue skies and follow the tracks of wolf, wolverine, marten and fox. Mountains, rivers, lakes and forests provide the backdrop for frequent sightings of caribou, moose and bear. Walker Lake sheds winter's mantle of ice in early June. Its turquoise waters run to depths of 700 feet. Fishermen will find aggressive lake trout, arctic char and grayling. You can fly-out to the Kobuk River for chum salmon and sheefish. Other guided activities are available, including sailing, hiking, bird and wildlife observation, and flightseeing. The friendly staff and customized service assure treasured memories of your Arctic adventure. **April-Sept.**

Alaska Wilderness Travel. 121 W. Fireweed, Anchorage, AK 99503. (907) 277-7671, 1-800-544-2236.

"GATES" BACKPACKING / NORTH FORK KOYUKUK KAYAKING

Located in North America's most remote mountains, the Central Brooks Range, the Gates of the Arctic National Park contains over 8 million acres of spectacular mountains, open tundra and boreal forests. After a bush plane fly-out from Fairbanks, you'll backpack 35-45 miles from the Arctic Divide to just above the "Gates," then continue on by Klepper kayak 135 miles down the north fork of the Koyukuk River to Bettles. Kleppers are stable and easy to paddle. They also allow you the independence to explore on your own. Good tasting, nutritious meals featuring whole grains and freshly baked breads and cakes are a highlight. **June-Sept.**

Alaska Wilderness Co-op. 4341 MacAlister Dr., Anchorage, AK 99515. (907) 243-3068.

Selawik
National Wildlife Refuge

Selawik straddles the Arctic Circle in northwestern Alaska. The refuge is composed of estuaries, lakes, river deltas, tundra slopes and an extensive system of tundra wetlands nestled between the Waring Mountains and the Selawik Hills. Selawik is located where the Bering Land Bridge once existed. Mastadon bones and those of bison, ancient caribou and horse are commonly found in the deep permafrost layers of the region.

Nearly half of all the bird species recorded in Alaska, including migratory waterbirds from six continents, are found in the Selawik region. Five percent of the Pacific Flyway's whistling swans nest here. Also found here is Alaska's densest population of loons. Shorebird species breed in such numbers as to eclipse all the other nesting birds combined. Foreign visitors, coming from as far away as Africa, India, China and Borneo include wheatears, bluethroats, arctic warblers and white and yellow wagtails. Probably the most magnificent migration is the annual flight of 300,000 snow geese that nest on Russia's Wrangell Island but stop to feed and rest in Selawik before heading south. Whooper swans from Asia occur in North America only at Selawik. Arctic terns come to nest from Antarctica. The Eskimo curlew (now probably extinct) once was common on Selawik marshes.

About one third of the 240,000 caribou of the Western Arctic herd winter in the taiga and tundra foothills of the Purcell and Waring Mountains. Other common mammals include moose, grizzly bear, wolves, coyotes and furbearers. Selawik is the northern limit of the ranges for Arctic hares and northern flying squirrels. Sheefish, whitefish, grayling, dolly varden, lake trout and northern pike are found here. Sheefish weighing 40 to 50 pounds are not uncommon.

The Selawik River provides good river rafting and sportfishing and portions have a National Wild and Scenic River designation. Kayaking on Hotham Inlet, west of the refuge, and on the brackish waters of Selawik Lake is an excellent way to see the refuge and its nesting birdlife. Inland areas offer good birdwatching on freshwater ponds, excellent berry picking and superb fishing. Access is by floatplane from Kotzebue.

Information: Refuge Manager, Selawik National Wildlife Refuge, PO Box 270, Kotzebue, AK 99752. (907) 442-3799.

Full moon in Selawik (FWS photo)

Photos by: (top and middle) MacGill Adams/ Wilderness Alaska; (bottom) Chuck Ash/ Hugh Glass Backpacking Co.

National Rivers

Congress established the National Wild and Scenic Rivers System to preserve in a relatively pristine condition rivers of unusual scenic, recreational, geologic, aquatic, riparian, historic or cultural value. All or part of 25 such rivers in Alaska are designated Wild and Scenic.

These rivers are classified as Wild (most restricted use), Scenic (less restricted use) and Recreational (least restricted use). They are administered by the National Park Service, the U.S. Fish and Wildlife Service and the Bureau of Land Management.

For use and access information, contact the park, refuge, or administrative unit in which the river is located. These agencies are as follows: **Alagnak** (Katmai National Park), **Alatna** (Gates of the Arctic National Park), **Andreafsky** (Yukon Delta National Wildlife Refuge), **Aniakchak** (Aniakchak National Park), **Beaver Creek** (Bureau of Land Management), **Birch Creek** (Bureau of Land Management), **Charley** (Yukon-Charley National Park), **Chilikadrotna** (Lake Clark National Park and Preserve), **Delta** (Bureau of Land Management), **Forty-mile** (Bureau of Land Management), **Gulkana** (Bureau of Land Management), **Ivishak** (Arctic National Wildlife Reserve), **John** (Gates of the Arctic National Park), **Kobuk** (Gates of the Arctic National Park), **Mulchatna** (Lake Clark National Park), **Noatak** (Gates of the Arctic National Park and Preserve), **North Fork Koyukuk** (Gates of the Arctic National Park and Preserve), **Nowitna** (Nowitna National Wildlife Refuge), **Salmon** (Kobuk Valley National Park), **Selawik** (Selawik National Wildlife Refuge), **Sheenjek** (Arctic National Wildlife Refuge), **Tinaguk** (Gates of the Arctic National Park and Preserve), **Tlikakila** (Lake Clark National Park), **Unalakleet** (Bureau of Land Management), **Wind** (Arctic National Wildlife Refuge).

Takeout on the John River. (MacGill Adams photo/Wilderness Alaska)

Gary Goodson

KILLIK-COLVILLE, NIGU-ETIVULUK-COLVILLE RIVER TRIPS

The Killik and the Nigu are two of the North Slope's most scenic rivers. You'll spend several days in the mountainous headwaters of the Killik before following its course down to ever-widening vistas. Wildlife abounds, and many of the mountain Eskimos (Nunamiut) from Anaktuvuk Pass trap wolves, fox, lynx and wolverine here in the winter. Arctic sand dunes line the riverbanks as do myriads of wildflowers. Below Sunday Rapids, many of the rock outcroppings are rich in fossils. Upon your arrival at Umiat, you'll fly back to the "land of the trees," south of the Brooks. An alternate route to the Colville is the scenic Nigu-Etivuluk river drainage. Here you are the only visitor. Caribou, grizzly and wolves are frequently seen. Fishing is good for trout, arctic char and grayling. **May-Sept.**

Alaska Wilderness Co-op. 4341 MacAlister Drive, Anchorage, AK 99515. (907) 243-3068.

Dave Schmitz

BROOKS RANGE DOGSLEDDING

Longer hours of sunlight and higher daytime temperatures make February and March an ideal time for dogsledding in the Arctic. As you travel broad boreal valleys clothed in their deep mantle of powder snow, you'll learn to hook up, feed, and drive the dog teams. After an invigorating day of exploring, snowshoeing, skiing, or tracking, you'll be delighted at the sight of the snug trapline cabin or heated wall tent where you can enjoy the crisp starry evenings with their panoramic displays of shimmering, colorful northern lights. There's good food and plenty of it, since you require more calories in the colder weather. Excellent physical conditioning is required to enjoy these trips to the fullest, as a dogsled trip does not always mean riding the sled. Winter trips are very personalized and are limited to one to four persons. **Nov-March.**

Brooks Range Wilderness Trips. PO Box 48A, Bettles, AK 99726. (907) 692-5312.

SHEENJEK RIVER TRIP

Your trip begins in Fairbanks where a bush plane will take you to the headwaters of the Sheenjek at Last Lake in the eastern Brooks Range. Here you'll start your gentle but fast raft descent of Class I water with occasional Class II-III whitewater. On your l5-day trip you'll traverse three different Arctic ecosystems, from mountain-rimmed tundra meadows down through spruce-poplar-birch forests and into the broad meandering river plain of the Yukon Flats. The fall season allows you to enjoy the changing colors of the alpine tundra, boreal forests and taiga and to observe the movement of mammals and migration of birds. Your take-out is at Fort Yukon. **Aug-Sept.**

Alaska Wilderness Co-op. 4341 MacAlister Drive, Anchorage, AK 99515. (907) 243-3068.

Kobuk Valley
National Park

Even though the Kobuk Valley lies well above the Arctic Circle, a summer visitor might well mistake portions of it for an equatorial desert. Over one-tenth of the valley, some 300 square miles, is covered by sun-baked sand. The Great Kobuk Sand Dunes consist of 25 square miles of shifting dunes where summer temperatures can exceed 100°F (37°C). It is the world's largest active dune field in Arctic latitudes.

The dry, predominantly cold climate of the Kobuk Valley still approximates that of late Pleistocene times, supporting a remnant of the flora (including sage brush and beach rye grass) once covering the vast Arctic steppe bridging Alaska and Asia. Herds of caribou crossing the Kobuk River at Onion Portage have been hunted by the Eskimo people since 1250 A.D. In fact, the date of human occupation at the portage goes back 12,500 years, forming a benchmark by which other arctic archeological sites are measured. The park's 1.7 million acres remain an important area for traditional subsistence harvest of moose, bear, caribou, fish, waterfowl, and many alimentary and medicinal plants.

Both the Kobuk and Salmon rivers which run through the park offer easy canoeing and kayaking.

Two airlines offer jet service from Anchorage and Fairbanks to Kotzebue. Scheduled air service is available from Kotzebue to nearby villages and local air and boat charter is available by advance arrangement.

Information: Superintendent, Kobuk Valley National Park, PO Box 287, Kotzebue, AK 99752. (907) 271-4243.

Crossing the Great Kobuk Sand Dunes (NPS photo)

KOBUK RIVER VALLEY & THE GREAT SAND DUNES

Paddle and float the Kobuk River from the village of Ambler along the picturesque southwest flank of the Brooks Range to Kiana. Fast changing fall colors, abundant berries, plentiful wildlife and the movements of caribou through the region provide a variety of daily sights and activities. The flora, fauna and geology of the Kobuk River Valley, with its intertwining tundra and taiga environments, are unusually diverse. At Ikavet Creek you'll backpack to the Great Kobuk Sand Dunes and camp at the edge of 25 square miles of active dune fields. Animal tracks, varied flora, and scattered dead trees among the tannish-white sand provide unusual photographic settings in morning and evening light. You'll also have plenty of time to fish, explore and hunt for fossil ivory and jade pebbles. **Aug. 9-23.**

Alaska Wilderness Co-op. 4341 MacAlister Drive, Anchorage, AK 99515. (907) 243-3068.

ARRIGETCH BACKPACKING / UPPER KOBUK FISHING & KAYAKING

Arrigetch means "fingers of the hand extended," an apt description for this unique group of Central Brooks Range peaks in the Gates of the Arctic National Park. You'll spend 10 days backpacking 55 miles through the backside of the Arrigetch Peaks. The backpacking is difficult, but the rewards, including views of a 3,000-foot sheer granite wall rising from grassy meadows, are many. A dozen hidden valleys beckon for further exploration. Few people ever venture here. You'll spend the next 10 days Klepper kayaking and fishing 135 miles down the upper Kobuk River to the village of Kobuk, the uppermost village on the river. You'll fish for grayling, northern pike, lake trout and the world famous sheefish or "Tarpon of the North". **Aug.**

Alaska Wilderness Travel. 121 W. Fireweed, Anchorage, AK 99503. (907) 277-7671, 1-800-544-2236.

ALATNA RIVER KAYAKING

This trip begins with a flight from Fairbanks to the town of Bettles, located above the Arctic Circle, and then takes you to the Gates of the Arctic National Park. You will spend a week backpacking 35 miles through the Arrigetch Peaks, exploring some of the less-visited valleys. One of your stops will be at a hot springs where Dall sheep are frequently seen. Following this, you'll enjoy a leisurely week of kayaking through the Alatna River Valley. If water levels allow, you will paddle an upper stretch of the river--a section few people get to see. No previous river experience is necessary, as Kleppers (a very stable German-built folding kayak) are used. Single and double Kleppers are available. **Aug.**

Alaska Wilderness Travel. 121 W. Fireweed, Anchorage, AK 99503. (907) 277-7671, 1-800-544-2236.

Arctic

Noatak
National Preserve

Noatak National Preserve protects the largest untouched river basin in the United States. The Noatak River runs above the Arctic Circle from glacial melt atop Mount Igikpak (8,570 feet), the highest point in the Brooks Range, out to Kotzebue Sound. Along its 685-kilometer (425-mile) course it has carved out the Grand Canyon of the Noatak. This striking, scenic canyon serves as a migration route for plants and animals between subarctic and arctic environments. In recognition of its pristine beauty and ecological significance, UNESCO has made the Noatak River basin an International Biosphere Reserve.

The Noatak serves as a natural highway not only for plants and animals, but also for wilderness travelers. The preserve is especially suited for canoeing and kayaking because the river is slow moving and gentle along most of its course. Only at its headwaters is the Noatak rough. Backpacking in the foothills here is also an attractive recreational opportunity. Among the preserve's large mammals are grizzly and black bear, caribou, wolves, lynx, and many Dall sheep. There is also a high concentration of birds in the preserve's 6.5 million acres, as summer brings migratory birds to the Noatak basin from Asia and the tip of South America. The river itself supports arctic char, whitefish, grayling and salmon.

Visitors can reach the preserve by charter flights out of Kotzebue and Bettles-Evansville, which are served by scheduled airlines from Fairbanks or Anchorage.

Information: Superintendent, Noatak National Preserve, PO Box 287, Anchorage, AK 99752. (907) 271-4243.

High country of the upper Noatak (David Ketscher photo/ Sourdough Outfitters)

NOATAK HEADWATERS BACKPACKING

This trek amidst towering peaks, small hanging glaciers, and incomparable wilderness is for the experienced backpacker. After a dropoff near Walker Lake, you'll hike among the highest peaks in the central and western Brooks Range, including 8,800-foot Mt. Igikpak. You'll cross over from the Kobuk to the Noatak River drainage, fishing, photographing and enjoying this vast wilderness along the way. You may also take a journey down the Noatak, one of the most majestic rivers in the world. Your guides are longtime Alaskans with extensive arctic experience. Winners of the Alaska Visitors Association "Heart of Gold" award for extra warm hospitality, they have a client return rate of over 50 percent. Your trip begins in Bettles, an historic supply point for Arctic miners and resident Natives. **Late June.**

Alaska Wilderness Travel. 121 W. Fireweed, Anchorage, AK 99503. (907) 277-7671, 1-800-544-2236.

NOATAK RIVER CANOEING

Born in the melting snows of the Brooks Range and running 400 miles west to Kotzebue Sound, the magnificent Noatak River lies completely above the Arctic Circle. This premier adventure begins with a bush plane fly-out from Bettles, followed by a three-week float of the river's entire 400-mile length. You'll pass through an amazing variety of geographic settings--jagged Arctic mountains, treeless tundra plains, steep canyons and finally into the spruce forest. Near Kotzebue Sound, you'll meet Natives of the village of Noatak, the only settlement along the entire river. And of course, there will be plenty of time for hiking and fishing for grayling, northern pike, arctic char, salmon and lake trout. Shorter trips taking in only portions of the Noatak are also available. **June-Aug.**

Alaska Wilderness Co-op. 4341 MacAlister Drive, Anchorage, AK 99515. (907) 243-3068.

Permafrost

Any layer of ground continuously frozen for over 2 years is considered to be permafrost. In the summer permafrost helps transform Arctic Alaska from what would otherwise be a desert into lush wetlands and tundra plains filled with wildlife. The permafrost keeps what scant precipitation falls here close to the surface, creating thousands of ponds and lakes and a plentiful water supply for plants.

The seasonal freezing and melting of fissures in the permafrost create the characteristic polygon patterns of arctic tundra. A related process causes silt-filled ponds to expand into circular mounds (often surrounded by a ring of differentiated vegetation) called pingos. The formation of some pingos has been dated back 4,000 years.

FWS photo

Cape Krusenstern
National Monument

Changing seas levels and the action of wind and waves over time have formed 113 lateral beach ridges at Cape Krusenstern National Monument. Extending from the mainland out into the Chukchi Sea, these successive gravel ridges provide chronologically ordered evidence of 5,000 years of marine mammal hunting by Eskimo peoples. Artifacts from nearby creek bluffs date back 6,000 years and provide a benchmark for dating each of the cape's more recent beach ridges with their accompanying evidence of human habitation.

As old living sites became landbound by the shoreline's seaward advance, the Eskimo abandoned their tents and sod houses to establish new camps nearer the sea. This process has continued ever since Arctic Eskimos first turned to the sea for subsistence. The Eskimo still hunt seals along the cape's outermost beach. With rifles instead of traditional harpoons they hazard spring ice floes to take "oogruk," or bearded seal. At shoreline campsites the women trim and render the catch for the hides, meat, and seal oil still vital to their subsistence.

Visitors can arrange chartered aircraft and boats out of Kotzebue, which has daily commercial service from Anchorage and Fairbanks.

Information: Superintendent, Cape Krusenstern National Monument, PO Box 287, Kotzebue, AK 99752. (907) 271-4243.

Remnants of ancient Native pit houses (NPS photo)

NOME / KOTZEBUE TOUR

Recent history and a very ancient past are combined in this Arctic Circle tour of Nome and Kotzebue. In Nome, a colorful gold-rush town founded in 1898, you can experience the thrill of panning for gold on the same beaches that once yielded millions to 20,000 fortune seekers at the turn of the century. Traveling above the Arctic Circle to Kotzebue, an Eskimo trading center for 6,000 years, you'll discover an ancient culture. You'll see racks of drying fish, whale and walrus meat. You'll watch traditional dances depicting Eskimo life and history, shop for authentic Native handicrafts made of ivory, gold and jade and perhaps participate in a Native celebration or join in an Eskimo blanket toss. Two and three day package tours are available. **June-Sept.**

Alaska Wilderness Travel. 121 W. Fireweed, Anchorage, AK 99503. (907) 277-7671, 1-800-544-2236.

NPS

Alaska's Natives

Before Western colonization, Alaska's Eskimos, Indians and Aleuts traded and fought with each other--taking slaves, plunder and territory--but inhabited separate regions. The Aleuts lived in the Aleutian Islands and on the Alaska Peninsula; the Inupiaq and Yupik Eskimo lived along Alaska's northern and western coasts; the Athabascan Indians populated the interior regions; and the Tlingit, Haida and Tsimshian Indians lived along Alaska's southeastern coast.

Today ethnic and territorial distinctions have blurred considerably (especially among 13,000 Alaskans of Native ancestry living in urban areas), but most of the state's 64,000 Natives still live on traditional lands. Much remains of these cultures though Westernization has changed them dramatically. New diseases and forced relocations under Russian rule reduced the Aleut population from 15,000 to 900 by 1848. The introduction of rum, molasses and bounty hunting by Russian, English and American traders resulted in the disintegration of traditional Native economies and living patterns. Christian missionaries introduced teachings which supplanted traditional beliefs.

In 1971 the U.S. government made Alaska's Natives shareholders of corporations which received land and money in settlement of aboriginal land claims that had blocked development of Alaska's oil fields. While these entitlements have done much to increase political influence, cultural pride and economic opportunity for some, the loss of traditional lands which may result from corporate failures is now a growing concern.

Arctic
National Wildlife Refuge

The Arctic National Wildlife Refuge, or ANWR (an-whar) as it is now commonly called, encompasses one of the most spectacular assemblages of arctic plants, wildlife and geological land forms in the world. Next to the mountains of Greenland's icecap, the sawtooth ridges and tall peaks of the eastern Brooks Range which bisect ANWR are the tallest peaks in the Arctic. ANWR is home to free-roaming herds of caribou and musk ox which were reintroduced to the refuge in 1969 after being eradicated by whaling crews and the Eskimo in the 1850's. Dall sheep, packs of wolves and solitary species such as wolverine, the barren-ground grizzly bear and polar bear which den on ANWR's coastal plain are also found here. Offshore, beluga whales, seals and the endangered bowhead whale feed in the many estuaries and lagoons of the Beaufort Sea coast.

Summer on the refuge is brief and intense. Arctic-adapted plants flourish even though permafrost is within 1.5 feet of the surface. It may take 300 years for a white spruce at tree line to reach a diameter of five inches; small willow shrubs may be 50 to 100 years old.

ANWR's tundra plain and vast wetlands draw breeding birds from four continents, including sandhill cranes, swans and 250,000 snow geese from Russia's Wrangell Island and Canada's MacKenzie Delta which rendezvous here in late August to rest and feed.

The refuge protects the entire Alaska portion of the Porcupine caribou herd's feeding, calving and migration territory. With over 100,000 animals this is one of the two largest herds in Alaska.

Use of ANWR is increasing. Activities include float trips on the Ivishak, Sheenjek and Wind rivers (all part of the Wild and Scenic River System), hiking, backpacking the uplands and river headwaters of the Brooks Range, hunting, fishing for grayling, pike, arctic char and lake trout, and wildlife observation. Barter Island is the closest settlement to the refuge and is serviced by regular flights from Fairbanks.

Information: Refuge Manager, Arctic National Wildlife Refuge, Federal Building and Courthouse, Box 20, 101-12th Street, Fairbanks, AK 99701. (907) 456-0250.

Musk ox grazing beneath the Franklin Mountains (Ron Yarnell photo / Wilderness: Alaska/Mexico)

Ted Swem

MacGill Adams

BIRDING IN THE ARCTIC NATIONAL WILDLIFE REFUGE

The Arctic National Wildlife Refuge is home to a variety of shorebirds, waterfowl, gyrfalcons, jaegers, snowy owls, eiders, and perhaps some species as yet undiscovered there. The last accepted sighting of the Eskimo curlew was made in the Refuge a few years ago. You can try for the next record! Starting high in the mountains of the Brooks Range you will float north through successive ecological zones, across the vast coastal plain and on to the Arctic Ocean. On the way you'll take time to hike and enjoy the plentiful wildlife. The Porcupine caribou herd (160,000 animals) migrate to this coastal plain to calve. Now is the time to see this unique wilderness; it may never be the same once attempts to open the coastal plain for oil development intensify. Trips offered **June-Aug.**

Wilderness Birding Adventures. PO Box 103747, Anchorage, AK 99510-3747. (907) 694-7442.

BROOKS RANGE TRANSECT BACKPACK

From Fairbanks you'll fly to Barter Island, a small Eskimo village on the Arctic Ocean, where a charter pilot will take you to the high mountains. Landing within sight of the continental divide, you'll hike down hills and across valleys through an ecosystem frantically condensing vital reproduction into the short summer. The rapid-fire rate of change creates a striking effect much like time-lapse photography. The hills will be awash in wildflowers, Jackson Pollock-style, and the tundra explosive with nesting birds. The sun hangs continuously overhead. Your chances of seeing Dall sheep, grizzly, moose, red fox and wolves are excellent. If the timing is right, you'll see the post-calving aggregation of the migrating Porcupine caribou herd. You'll have plenty of time to explore, photograph, or reflect in a tranquility rare on this earth. **June.**

Wilderness Alaska. 6710 Potter Heights, Anchorage, AK 99516. (907) 345-3366.

KONGAKUT RIVER PADDLE RAFTING

In the arctic, spring is short and intense. Everpresent sunlight incises the wilderness traveler with boundless energy to explore. You will be in the mountains during the entire length of this trip and will have ample time for hiking. If you are lucky, you'll have the chance to see hundreds of caribou swimming the river as the Porcupine herd makes its spring migration through this area. On the open tundra chances are good of spotting other arctic animals as well, especially Dall sheep and grizzly bear. Fishing for arctic char and grayling, walking among the spring wildflowers, and running an exciting stretch of whitewater will add to your experiences in this remote northeast corner of Alaska. **Mid June.**

Alaska Wilderness Co-op. 4341 MacAlister Dr., Anchorage, AK 99515. (907) 243-3068.

Western

Western Alaska is a remote sparsely populated area stretching along the Bering Sea from the Arctic Circle to Bristol Bay. Western is probably the least visited region in the state. Travel to this region is generally possible only by plane, and distances and light use of these air routes make fares more expensive. Those who travel to Western Alaska will find a vast, undiscovered and pristine land filled with some of the world's greatest natural wonders.

This is the land of the Yupik Eskimo who have preserved an ancient subsistence culture. To the south and east the highlands of Lake Clark National Park and Preserve provide spawning grounds which help make the Bristol Bay red salmon fishery the worlds largest. Along the southern coast Togiak National Wildlife Refuge holds some of the world's largest seabird nesting colonies and provides a base for the only viewing of walrus "haul outs" in North America. Inland from Togiak lies Wood-Tikchik State Park, the nation's largest state park.

North of Togiak lies Yukon Delta National Wildlife Preserve, the nation's largest refuge and one of the world's most important water bird habitats. The refuge also includes Nunivak Island with its rare musk ox herd.

North of the Yukon Delta and inland is Innoko National Wildlife Refuge. This refuge holds one of the world's densest black bear populations and produces the state's greatest yields of beaver. The Iditarod Trail also winds along its western boundary, then turns west to the Seward Peninsula and runs to the historic gold rush town of Nome. The Bering Land Bridge National Preserve lies along the northern coast of the peninsula and preserves flora, fauna and artifacts dating back to the first appearance of people in the Americas.

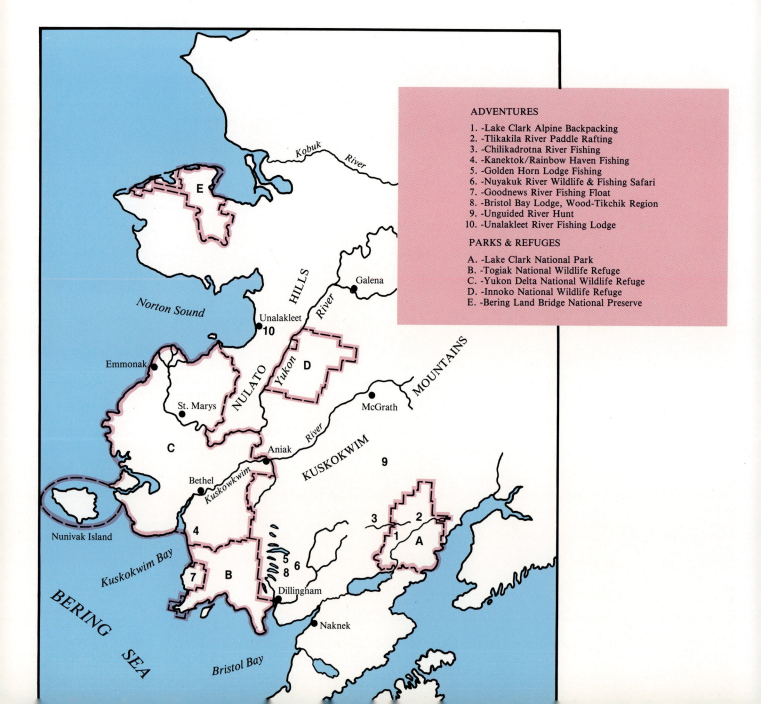

ADVENTURES

1. -Lake Clark Alpine Backpacking
2. -Tlikakila River Paddle Rafting
3. -Chilikadrotna River Fishing
4. -Kanektok/Rainbow Haven Fishing
5. -Golden Horn Lodge Fishing
6. -Nuyakuk River Wildlife & Fishing Safari
7. -Goodnews River Fishing Float
8. -Bristol Bay Lodge, Wood-Tikchik Region
9. -Unguided River Hunt
10. -Unalakleet River Fishing Lodge

PARKS & REFUGES

A. -Lake Clark National Park
B. -Togiak National Wildlife Refuge
C. -Yukon Delta National Wildlife Refuge
D. -Innoko National Wildlife Refuge
E. -Bering Land Bridge National Preserve

Rainbow over Wood-Tikchik lakes region (A. J. Hand photo/Bristol Bay Lodge)

Western

Lake Clark
National Park and Preserve

The mountains of Lake Clark National Park and Preserve have been described as "the Alaskan Alps." Jagged peaks, the plumes of active volcanos, waterfalls tumbling down sheer granite walls to turquoise waters far below, lush maritime rain forests, high rolling tundra hills with crystaline lakes and streams make this an area not easily susceptible to comparison. Here caribou calve and brown bear fish teeming runs of red salmon.

The Chigmit mountains along Cook Inlet's western shore join the Aleutian and Alaska ranges and divide the park and preserve into two distinct regions: the forested coastal plain and the drier tundra hills of the lake country to the west. Lake Clark, fed by hundreds of waterfalls cascading from surrounding mountains, is part of an important red salmon spawning ground, at times providing over half of the Bristol Bay run which is the world's largest.

The Lake Clark area is a border land between the territories of the western (Yupik) Eskimo, the Aleuts and the Tanaina Indians and has historically been both a trade route and a battle ground. The park and preserve contain 3.7 million acres.

Only one hour's flight from Anchorage by small plane, the park is also accessible via air charter out of Kenai or Iliamna. Lodging is available from private operators within the park and preserve, and facilities range from primitive to plush.

Information: Superintendent, Lake Clark National Park and Preserve, 701 C Street, Box 61, Anchorage, AK 99513. (907) 271-4243.

Fishing on Lake Clark (Carla Jones photo/ Arctic Brotherhood & Entertainment Committee)

LAKE CLARK ALPINE BACKPACKING

This week-long trek through alpine terrain will begin with a float plane fly-in from Anchorage to Turquoise Lake at the headwaters of the Mulchatna River. Your backpacking route will take you southward along the western flanks of the Chigmit Mountains, over a mountain pass and down to Twin Lakes at the headwaters of the Chilikadrotna River. You will spend a week hiking and camping as you travel this little-known wilderness with its rugged snow-capped peaks, glacially contoured terrain, alpine streams and lakes and diverse varieties of flora and fauna. Your pick-up point is Twin Lakes from which you'll fly back to Point Alsworth and then back to Anchorage via the rugged and beautiful Lake Clark Pass. **August.**

Alaska Treks N Voyages. PO Box 600-K, Moose Pass, AK 99631. (907) 288-3610 or 224--3960.

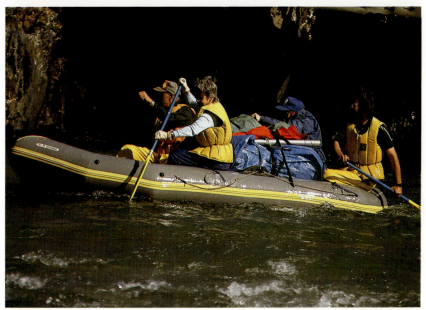

TLIKAKILA RIVER PADDLE RAFTING

Your trip begins with a spectacular flight through Lake Clark Pass. Beyond each wing tip, you'll see waterfalls and the blue ice of hanging glaciers on the jagged peaks of the Chigmit Mountains. You will float the entire length of the Tlikakila, beginning at its headwaters in the pass. Flanked by meadows of fireweed and lupine and evergreen forests, the Tlikakila flows swiftly down its narrow valley. Although not difficult to run, several rapids make the descent exciting and everyone shares in the fun of paddling. Your attention is frequently drawn upward to the icefalls, waterfalls and perpendicular rock faces surrounding you. Your trip through one of Alaska's most scenic wild rivers ends at the turquoise waters of Lake Clark. **July.**

Alaska Wilderness Travel. 121 W. Fireweed, Anchorage, AK 99503. (907) 277-7671, 1-800-544-2236.

CHILIKADROTNA RIVER FISHING

The turquoise waters of the Twin Lakes in the heart of Lake Clark National Park are the put-in for this five day fishing adventure. You'll enjoy an alpine hike and picnic while your guides set up rafts for your descent through the Alaska Range on this nationally designated Wild and Scenic River. Fishing can be excellent in season for salmon, trout, dolly varden, and grayling, and hiking is good throughout the trip. You'll want to keep an eye out for moose, bear, eagle, and beaver. This trip is completely outfitted and you will be provided with your own guiding jacket for an extra level of comfort. Menus include prime rib and, if your luck is good, fresh barbecued salmon. **June-Sept.**

Alaska Wilderness Co-op. 4341 MacAlister Dr., Anchorage, AK 99515. (907) 243-3068.

Western

Togiak
National Wildlife Refuge

Togiak lies between Kuskokwim and Bristol bays in southwestern Alaska. No area of equivalent size in Alaska can boast a greater variety of wildlife. The tundra slopes of the Ahklun Mountains make up 80 percent of the refuge. The topography includes mountain crags, fast-flowing rivers, deep lakes, marshy lowlands, ponds, estuaries, coastal lagoons, sea cliffs and miles of sand and gravel beaches. Interior forests reach their southwestern limits here.

Togiak is a breeding and resting area for waterfowl and shorebirds returning from wintering areas in Russia, Japan, Mexico, South America, New Zealand, and the South Pacific. The refuge includes the world-renowned cliffs at Cape Newenham and Cape Peirce which support what may be North America's largest seabird nesting colony. This rookery is estimated to hold as many as two million birds. Offshore waters are home to thousands of shearwaters, a pelagic bird that breeds south of the equator and never comes ashore while in North Pacific waters.

Small furbearers are found here but larger mammals are not abundant because of the lack of forest cover. Humpback, sperm, bowhead, finback, little piked and sei whales can be sighted in offshore seas. Four species of seal and a small sea lion herd forage near shore. Round Island (a small offshore island under state jurisdiction) is the only place in North America were one can witness the hauling out of walrus.

Some of the finest salmon and trout sport fishing waters in Alaska are in Togiak. Steelhead, dolly varden, grayling and char also challenge the angler. Some have called the Togiak River "the greatest natural sportfishing stream in America." River rafting is popular on the Kanektok and Togiak rivers. The refuge is accessible by charter from Dillingham.

Information: Refuge Manager, Togiak National Wildlife Refuge, PO Box 10201, Dillingham, AK 99576. (907) 842-1063.

Round Island walrus (D. Clive photo/FWS)

Bill Lyle

KANEKTOK / RAINBOW HAVEN FISHING

Surrounded by the Togiak National Wildlife Refuge, this virgin wilderness is accessible only by sea and air. The Kanektok River provides salmon fishing at its best. The average daily catch is 14 king salmon per person with many fish weighing up to 70 pounds. The average for silver salmon is over 30 per day per fisherman. Rainbow Haven has daily rainbow catches in the 6-12 pound range, world class grayling, and five salmon species. The rainbow and grayling fishery is strictly "catch and release." Flies and lures are used to catch these trophy-sized fish. Your camp features Weatherport steel-framed sleeping tents, cooking and dining tents, excellent kitchen fare, and hot showers for a comfortable and enjoyable outdoor experience. You can choose between six-person camps and four-person guided float trips. **June-Sept.**

Gone Fishing. William R. Lyle, PO Box 589, Wasilla, AK 99687. (907) 376-6514.

GOLDEN HORN LODGE FISHING

An angler's paradise awaits at Golden Horn Lodge, located in the Wood River/Tikchik Lakes region of Bristol Bay in southwest Alaska. This area offers you five types of salmon, rainbow trout, arctic char, dolly varden, arctic grayling, lake trout, and northern pike. You'll enjoy world class fishing in pristine wilderness, but that doesn't mean you'll be roughing it. All the luxuries await you at this "wilderness Hilton"--fine food, comfortable interiors, a crackling fire, and a well-stocked bar. Lavish menus include prime rib, New York Steak, baked salmon, homemade breads and pastries and fresh fruits. A fleet of planes and boats, as well as outcamps and expert guides assure guests the opportunity to enjoy scenery, wildlife, or the catch of a lifetime. **June-Sept.**

Golden Horn Lodge. PO Box 6748, Anchorage, AK 99502. (907) 243-1455.

NUYAKUK RIVER WILDLIFE / FISHING SAFARI

The Nuyakuk River, in Wood-Tikchik State Park, offers 50 miles of exceptional angling and wildlife viewing opportunities. In season you can fish for all five species of salmon as well as rainbow trout, char, grayling, and pike. Large comfortable rafts allow you to fish new waters each day. Photographers will want to bring a telephoto as moose, bear, beaver, and waterfowl may appear at any bend. Your guides are proficient in making wilderness travel comfortable, and you may enjoy fresh salmon barbecues and live music along the way. You'll take home your own guiding jacket and a video of your trip. Your trip departs from Anchorage and length is variable with 3-5 days recommended. **June-Sept.**

Alaska Wilderness Co-op. 4341 MacAlister Dr., Anchorage, AK 99515. (907) 243-3068.

Western

A. J. Hand

GOODNEWS RIVER FISHING FLOAT

This beautiful and unspoiled river threads its way through the Ahklun Mountains in the Togiak National Wildlife Refuge. From the headwaters lake to your take-out on the lower river, these emerald mountains are never far away. The river is serene and offers some of the finest fishing in Alaska. Up to 10 species of fish can be caught on a single float. The king salmon run is excellent with fish weighing up to 50 lbs. However, the real stars are the Goodnews silver salmon, which excel in number, size and freshness. Fishing is also excellent for rainbows, dollies, arctic char, grayling, and lake trout. Large tents and a portable riverside sauna will keep you comfortable all the way to the lower reaches of the river and your float plane rendezvous. **June-Oct.**

Alaska River & Ski Tours, Inc. 1831 Kuskokwim St., Suite 3, Anchorage, AK 99508. (907) 276-3418, Telex 25-147.

BRISTOL BAY LODGE, WOOD-TIKCHIK REGION

Ron and Maggie McMillan's lodge, in operation since 1972, offers you a world-class wilderness fishing experience. Located on a private in-holding of the vast Wood-Tikchik State Park, (the nation's largest state park), only 40 air miles north of Dillingham, the lodge provides casual elegance and comforts as well as superb fishing. Daily fly-out trips take you over scenic wilderness to the pristine habitat of 11 species of sportfish. The McMillans and their staff combine their experience and expertise to give you the angling experience of a lifetime. **June-Sept.**

Bristol Bay Lodge. PO Box 190349, Anchorage, AK 99519. (907) 248-1714.

UNGUIDED RIVER HUNT

This unguided trip is for the experienced outdoorsperson looking for a self-directed wilderness experience. Professional pilots with years of experience flying the Alaskan bush have learned the habits of moose, migrating caribou and other big game animals. During a familiarization fly-over, your pilot will point out several areas for game and terrain advantage before landing. After you've set up camp and overnighted, a fair-chase hunt can begin. Match your skill against the complexities of nature. This package includes a rubber raft and hip boots for shoreline hunting. You can bring your own tent, equipment and gear, or arrange for complete outfitting. **June-Sept.**

Alaska Wilderness Travel. 121 W. Fireweed, Anchorage, AK 99503. (907) 277-7671, 1-800-544-2236.

Yukon Delta
National Wildlife Refuge

The Yukon Delta is a broad, treeless wetland formed by the Yukon and Kuskokwim rivers and is famous for its plentiful birdlife. Its lakes, ponds, sloughs, meandering streams and land-locked river channels have never been inventoried, but estimates put their number at 500,000. Yukon Delta is the largest refuge in the nation--nearly the size of the state of Maine. Each spring, tens of millions of migrating waterfowl and shorebirds return to the Yukon Delta, making it one of the most important nesting and rearing regions in the world. Eighty percent of North America's whistling swans (30,000 birds) nest here. Spectacled eider and sandhill crane nest in major numbers. Nesting shorebirds number over 100 million.

Large game mammals inhabit the northern hills and eastern mountains. Four species of seal occur offshore and beluga whale swim up larger coastal rivers. Walrus also appear along the coast.

The refuge encompasses thirty-six Yupik Eskimo villages and is the heart of Yupik country. The legislation that established Yukon Delta enables rural residents to maintain a subsistence lifestyle.

The Nunivak Island portion of the refuge is visited by an array of Asian birds that rarely occur in North America, including the Mongolian plover, northern Middendorf's warbler, Japanese water pipit and Cassin's bullfinches, as well as the rare McKay's bunting. Nunivak's sea cliffs are home to some of the continent's largest pelagic bird rookeries. Although decimated by hunters by 1865, musk ox were reintroduced to Nunivak in 1931 from Greenland and have since been prolific. A transplant reindeer herd is also a major source of food and income for the island's Native residents. The herd is a particularly hardy strain since caribou bulls from Denali National Park were bred with local cows to produce a bigger, wilder herd.

Fishing and hunting here can be outstanding. The Andreafsky River is a nationally designated Wild and Scenic River. Its waters provide excellent fishing for salmon, char, grayling, northern pike and whitefish as well as good rafting possibilities. Other prime rivers for rafting and kayaking are the Atchuelinguk, Aniak and Kisarilik. Bethel is the largest settlement in the region and planes can be chartered here for further exploration of the Delta.

Information: Refuge Manager, Yukon Delta National Wildlife Refuge, PO Box 346, Bethel, AK 99559. (907) 543-3151.

Yukon Delta waterfowl nesting habitat (Spencer photo/FWS)

Innoko
National Wildlife Refuge

Innoko is composed of two unconnected sections totalling 4.25 million acres in the central Yukon River Valley. About 80% of the refuge consists of the Innoko River lowlands, a wetland of over 25,000 lakes and thousands of miles of sluggish oxbowed streams that provides waterfowl nesting habitat. Since Innoko lies in a transitional zone between the coastal tundra of Western Alaska and the boreal forests of the more eastern interior, it has a milder climate than most interior areas.

Innoko provides habitat for wolf, one of Alaska's densest black bear populations, grizzly bear, and the Beaver Mountain caribou herd which overwinters in the Innoko basin. The refuge is known for its beaver population. In some years, 40 percent of all beaver trapped in Alaska comes from the Koyukuk and Innoko river basins and 80 percent of that harvest comes from the Innoko region. The annual beaver harvest reaches 20,000 pelts.

A dense moose population is attributed to seasonal flooding along the streams which enhances the growth of willows -- the major winter browse of moose. Sometimes 50 or more moose can be seen feeding in a single willow stand. King, silver and chum salmon ascend the Yukon to Innoko. Subsistence fishers annually take over 300,000 salmon from area waters. Lakes and streams hold arctic grayling, whitefish, burbot, sheefish and northern pike.

A float trip on the Innoko River provides a convenient means to view wildlife, and fishing for northern pike is excellent. Sport hunting for moose and black bear is popular. The famed Iditarod Trail--a 1,200-mile dog musher's trail from Anchorage to Nome--traces the refuge's western boundary.

Information: Refuge Manager, Innoko National Wildlife Refuge, PO Box 69, McGrath, AK 99627. (907) 524-3251.

Beaver at work.
(FWS photo)

UNALAKLEET RIVER FISHING LODGE

Four hundred air miles northwest of Anchorage, far off the beaten path, is the Unalakleet River Fishing Lodge. Since the lodge is only 10 miles upriver from the Bering Sea, the fresh-run salmon found here are some of the strongest, hardest-fighting fish you'll ever encounter. The powerful and spirited ocean-fresh king salmon average 25-30 lbs., with some in the 50-60 lb. class. Silvers, dolly varden, trophy grayling and over a million pink salmon enter the Unalakleet River. Pinks take both lures and flies aggressively, earning them the reputation for striking "anything that hits the water." The main lodge, built of large handhewn spruce logs, overlooks the wild Unalakleet River Valley. Guests stay in fully modern, carpeted cabins on the river's edge. The lodge maintains a generous staff-to-guest ratio of one fishing guide per two clients. The dining is sumptuous. **June-Sept.**

Silvertip Lodges. PO Box 190389, Anchorage, AK 99519-0389. (907) 248-0419.

FWS

Musk Ox

The musk ox, or "oomingmak" (meaning "bearded one" in Eskimo), first evolved in Asia but was exterminated there by stone age hunters. Musk ox which had migrated across the Bering Land Bridge to America proliferated there until the 19th century when whalers, fur traders and the Eskimo totally decimated the continental herds. In 1931 a predecessor agency of the U.S. Fish & Wildlife Service transplanted musk ox from the only remaining population on Greenland to Alaska where they have since proliferated. Herds now have been established at Nunivak Island, Nelson Island, the Seward Peninsula, Cape Thompson, Cape Krusenstern, the North Slope, and in the Mat-Su Valley where they are raised commercially. Statewide, musk ox now number about 1,200.

Musk ox prefer arctic habitat where snowfall is 10 inches or less, making winter browse easily accessible. Males weigh up to 900 pounds, females up to 500 pounds. When threatened, a herd will back side-by-side into a circle protecting any young in the interior. Males, in turn, charge from this horned phalanx to challenge the invader and, if necessary, then retreat to the circle. The animal's name derives from reports by early explorers that in certain seasons it was too musky to eat.

Native businesses are experimenting with captive herds and have established the Oomingmak Musk Ox Producers' Cooperative. This cottage industry employs Native villagers who knit the oxen's soft cashmere-like underwool, called "qiviut," into scarves, sweaters and hats for sale to the public.

Western

Bering Land Bridge
National Preserve

Bering Land Bridge National Preserve is a remnant of the neck of land that bridged Asia and North America more than 13,000 years ago. It is believed to be part of the area where prehistoric Asian hunters entered the New World. The bridge itself is now overlain by the Chukchi and Bering seas. During the Ice Age, the preserve was part of a migration route for people, animals, and plants whenever ocean levels fell enough to expose the land bridge.

Today Eskimos in scattered villages, principally along the coast, pursue subsistence lifestyles and manage their reindeer herds in and around the preserve. Some 112 migratory bird species may be seen here, along with occasional seals, walrus, and whales. Grizzly bear, fox, wolf, and moose also inhabit the preserve. Other interesting features are rimless volcanoes called maar craters, the Serpentine Hot Springs, and seabird colonies at Sullivan Bluffs.

Air service out of Nome and Kotzebue is the usual means of access to this quite isolated area.

Information: Superintendent, Bering Land Bridge National Preserve, PO Box 220, Nome, AK 99762. (907) 271-4243.

*Reindeer pens
(Brett Coburn photo)*

Photos by: (top and middle) Golden Horn Lodge; (bottom) A.J. Hand/Bristol Bay Lodge.

Southwest

Southwest Alaska forms an arc stretching from the southwest mainland of Alaska far out into the Pacific past the international dateline. The mountainous Alaska Peninsula and the Aleutian Islands have been thrust up where the Pacific plate of the earth's crust is forcing its way under the North American plate. This tectonic activity also caused the formation of about 60 volcanos in the region. Southwest was the first part of the continent to become Russian America when Russian "promyshlenniki" or profiteers came here seeking furs in the 1700's. During the Japanese invasion of the Aleutians in WW II it became the first foreign occupied U. S. soil since the War of 1812.

Today the region is a sportfishing and hunting mecca. Kodiak Island and Kodiak National Wildlife Refuge were long known for having both the world's largest brown bears and its densest brown bear concentrations, although this has now changed with increased trophy hunting. The Alaska Peninsula National Wildlife Refuge now boasts the worlds densest concentrations of brown bear and also offers world record sport fish. Becharof National Wildlife Refuge and Katmai National Park and Preserve feature dramatic volcanic geology as well as world class concentrations of brown bear and salmon.

Aniakchak is a showpiece of the effects of geological forces and is probably the nation's most remote national park area. Izembek National Wildlife Refuge is internationally recognized as one of the world's most significant water bird habitats. The Alaska Maritime National Wildlife Refuge, an aggregation of widely scattered islands, protects significant habitats for birds and marine mammals. The Pribilof Islands, for example, hold the world's largest fur seal rookery and, in season, are the site of the world's largest aggregation of wild mammals.

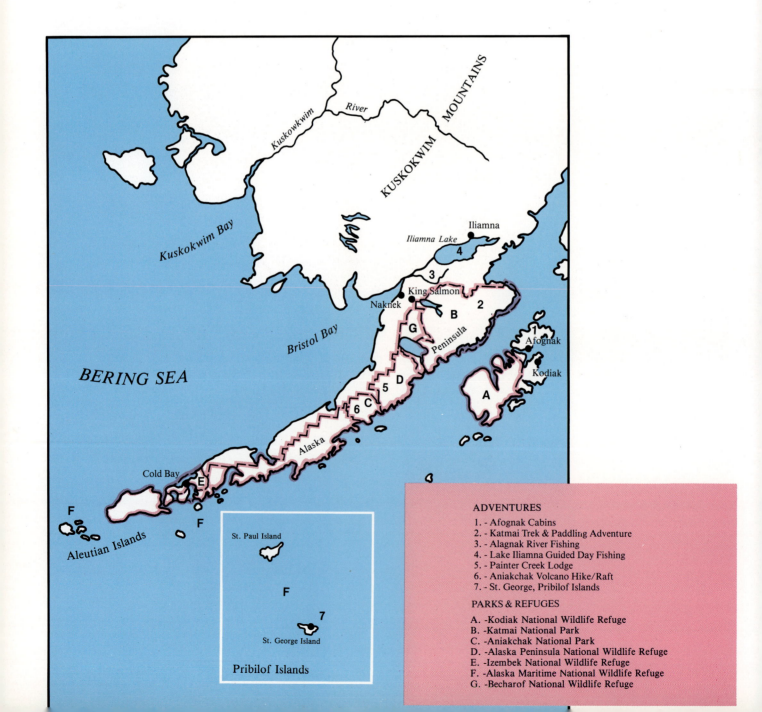

ADVENTURES

1. - Afognak Cabins
2. - Katmai Trek & Paddling Adventure
3. - Alagnak River Fishing
4. - Lake Iliamna Guided Day Fishing
5. - Painter Creek Lodge
6. - Aniakchak Volcano Hike/Raft
7. - St. George, Pribilof Islands

PARKS & REFUGES

A. - Kodiak National Wildlife Refuge
B. - Katmai National Park
C. - Aniakchak National Park
D. - Alaska Peninsula National Wildlife Refuge
E. - Izembek National Wildlife Refuge
F. - Alaska Maritime National Wildlife Refuge
G. - Becharof National Wildlife Refuge

Fishing off Afognak Island   (Peter Olsen photo/Afognak Cabins)

Kodiak
National Wildlife Refuge

The Kodiak refuge encompasses about two-thirds of Kodiak Island and a portion of Afognak Island to the north. Kodiak Island has an irregular coastline of bays, inlets and rugged mountains covered with coniferous forests and alpine vegetation. Spruce forests dominate the refuge. The interior is covered with lush, dense vegetation. Southwestern Kodiak is covered with hummocks (knolls) of grass. No place on the 100 by 40 mile island is more than 15 miles from the sea.

As well as being home to some of the world's largest brown bears, Kodiak also has one of the world's densest brown bear populations. Some 2,500 bears roam the refuge. Bears have poor eyesight but a keen sense of smell. When alarmed or curious, browns stand erect to get a better sniff of the intruder. Brown bear trails traverse the entire island. Bears traditionally step in the previous bear's tracks, wearing a trail that is a succession of deeply worn footprints--in some places two feet deep and hundreds of years old.

In addition to the brown bear, there are only five other indigenous land mammals on Kodiak: red fox, river otter, short-tailed weasel, little brown bat, and tundra vole. Black-tailed deer, beaver, muskrat, reindeer, mountain goat, Dall sheep and moose have been successfully introduced to the island.

Two hundred nesting pair of bald eagles reside year-round on the refuge. An estimated two million seabirds inhabit the coastal waters and nesting ducks inhabit refuge estuaries and lakes. The refuge also has a small peregrine falcon population. Whales, porpoises, seals, Steller's sea lions and sea otters live in offshore water.

Kodiak is known worldwide for brown bear hunting. Fishing is excellent for steelhead, dolly varden, rainbow trout and five species of salmon. The island is served by commercial flights and the state ferry system.

Information: Refuge Manager, Kodiak National Wildlife Refuge, PO Box 825, Kodiak, AK 99615. (907) 487-2600.

Brown bear surveying the terrain (Chuck Ash photo/ Hugh Glass Backpacking Co.)

Peter Olsen

John Fowler

AFOGNAK CABINS

Afognak Island, located 20 miles from Kodiak, lies at the northern fringe of the Sitka spruce range and is the world's only forest comprised solely of this tree specie. This rich habitat is home to a diverse array of wildlife including blacktail deer, the Kodiak bear, marten, fox and Alaska's only established elk herds. Salmon return annually to spawn here. Halibut, sea otter, puffin, seal and other marine birds and animals thrive in Afognak's bays and inlets. Whether you are hunting, fishing, hiking or seeking solitude, the Afognak Cabins will add greatly to the enjoyment of your visit. These large, cozy cabins sleep six and have oil stoves for cooking and heat. The avid outdoorsperson will enjoy the privacy and intrigue of this unguided adventure. **June-Dec.**

Afognak Cabins. 413 Rezanof Drive East, Kodiak, AK 99615. (907) 486-6014.

Russian America

Alaska was discovered in 1741 by Vitus Bering, a Dane commissioned by Peter the Great to help establish Russia as the first European power in the Pacific. In scope and difficulty Bering's trips across Siberia to Alaska easily overshadow the Lewis and Clark Expedition. Bering was followed by Russian "promyshlenniki," fur traders and profiteers who quickly subdued the Aleuts and set them to harvesting furs for trade with China.

Russia's colonization efforts in Alaska were never well backed, either with men or material. The colony's success in making do and fending off encroachments by the English and Americans is attributable largely to the Russian's shrewd and relatively humane treatment of Alaska's Natives. The Russians intermarried with the Aleuts and the Kenaitze Indians and enlisted them to help colonize and to fight the fierce Tlingit Indians of Southeast Alaska.

When the United States purchased Alaska from Russia in 1867 neither country wanted the exchange. Russian diplomats believed that the Americans would eventually take the territory by force and wanted to sell it before a confrontation developed. The United States entered into the exchange begrudgingly to repay Russia for being the only European power to actively support the Union during the Civil War. Upon learning of the sale, the Russian public expressed outrage. Even after the deal had closed, Congress considered backing out under pressure from the American press which claimed that Alaska's furs, timber, fish and minerals were worthless and that the land itself was "unfit for civilized men."

Southwest

Becharof
National Wildlife Refuge

Becharof lies between Katmai National Park and Preserve and the Alaska Peninsula Refuge. The refuge is dominated by Becharof Lake which, at 458 square miles, is the second largest lake in Alaska. The lake is surrounded by low rolling hills, tundra wetlands, and volcanic peaks. The Gas Rocks area, on the slopes of 5,000-foot Mt. Peulik, include some of the few known volcanic maar craters in the world and make it a prime area for study of recent volcanic activity.

The red salmon spawning streams attract one of the largest concentrations of brown bear in Alaska. From mid-July to September several hundred bears will be fishing on all the streams along the lake's south shore. In the fall when denning begins, most brown bears prefer to dig their dens on north facing slopes with plenty of undergrowth. Becharof's bears prefer to make their dens at Island Lake (the southeastern arm of Becharof Lake), and on the offshore islands, only a few feet above the shoreline. This lowland bear denning is unique to Becharof; 232 dens surround the shoreline and 14 are on the islands. Moose inhabit the refuge in moderate numbers and about 10,000 caribou of the Alaska Peninsula herd winter on the refuge. Other mammals include wolves, wolverines, river otters, red fox and beaver. In addition, thousands of sea mammals such as sea otters, sea lions, harbor seals, and migratory whales inhabit the shoreline.

Becharof Lake and its tributaries contribute over four million salmon annually to the Bristol Bay fishery. Rainbow trout, arctic char, and grayling flourish on the refuge. Waterfowl are common in the wetlands and coastal estuaries while nesting eagles, peregrine falcons, and thousands of sea birds inhabit the sea cliffs and islands. Some 80,000 nesting seabirds make Paule Bay in the southern part of the refuge home to the largest marine bird colonies on the Alaskan Peninsula mainland.

Becharof offers outstanding bear and caribou hunting. Trophy-sized rainbow trout, arctic char, grayling and salmon are found here. A half-day hiking trip from Fish Village (on Becharof's southeast shore) leads up through a mountain pass and down to the abandoned Aleut coastal village of Kanatak. Kayaking possibilities exist on the lake itself and on the Shelikof Strait coastline from Portage Bay to Cape Kekurnoi. Access to the refuge is by floatplane from King Salmon.

Information: Refuge Manager, Becharof National Wildlife Refuge, PO Box 277, King Salmon, AK 99613. (907) 246-3339.

Gulls eyeing brown bear's salmon catch (Kris Cassity photo)

Photos by Peter Olsen/Afognak Cabins.

Southwest

Katmai
National Park and Preserve

In 1912 a tremendous volcano erupted in an unexplored wilderness that today is Katmai National Park and Preserve. The blast was one of the most violent ever recorded, expelling no less than 2.5 cubic miles of ash. These fine particles so obscured the atmosphere that the entire North American continent was cooled for a season. Afterwards, in what would become known as the Valley of Ten Thousand Smokes, a bed of lava 15 miles long, 3 to 6 miles wide and 700 feet deep formed. Fumaroles by the millions issued steam hot enough to melt zinc. Today, only a few active vents remain.

Katmai's scenic menu boasts lakes, rivers, glaciers, waterfalls, and a lush coastline of plunging cliffs and islets covering some 3.9 million acres. This area is home to the Alaska brown bear, which can weigh up to 1,200 pounds from gorging on salmon abundant here. Katmai has some of southwestern Alaska's best trophy sportfishing, including large red (sockeye) salmon runs.

Scheduled jets from Anchorage serve King Salmon on the park's west side. From June through Labor Day daily commercial flights operate between King Salmon and Brooks Lodge. Air charters from King Salmon or Iliamna are available from May through October.

Information: Superintendent, Katmai National Park and Preserve, PO Box 7, King Salmon, AK 99613. (907) 271-4243.

Red salmon moving up spawning stream. (NPS photo)

Chuck Ash

KATMAI TREK & PADDLE ADVENTURE

Katmai is a national park with two very geographically distinct regions. The eastern portion encompasses the peaks and glaciers of the Aleutian Range, a young range which is still forming. In 1912 the volcanic convulsions of this range created the Valley of 10,000 Smokes. The trekking portion of your adventure takes place amid this geologic splendor. During the last ice age, glaciers from these same mountains ground their way many miles to the west. When the ice age waned huge ice-scoured depressions remained. Meltwater filled these basins to create the extensive lake system of western Katmai. These lakes are now the cradle for a rich and diverse ecosystem. Spawning salmon are the crucial link in the ecological web of Katmai. The paddling portion of your adventure takes place on the clear waters of these lakes. **July-Aug.**

**Hugh Glass Backpacking Co.
PO Box 110796-AB, Anchorage, AK 99511.
(907) 243-1922.**

ALAGNAK RIVER FISHING

A raft trip down the nationally designated Wild and Scenic Alagnak River in Katmai National Park offers not only beautiful scenery, but exceptional angling opportunities--from the powerful, deep runs of king salmon to the tailwalking acrobatics of reds, silvers and rainbows. Although the five salmon species are the main attraction, trophy rainbow and lake trout, dolly varden, grayling, and pike are also available. Photo opportunities are plentiful. Keep your camera ready for brown bear, moose, beaver, otter, and swans. Your guides are adept at adding the creature comforts to wilderness travel, sometimes including fresh salmon barbecues and live music along the way. You'll take home a comfortable guiding jacket and a video capturing some of your trip's highlights. Your trip departs from Anchorage and will last 4-6 days. **June-Sept.**

Alaska Wilderness Co-op. 4341 MacAlister, Anchorage, AK 99515. (907) 243-3068.

LAKE ILIAMNA GUIDED DAY FISHING

You will be one of the relatively few people who experience magnificent Lake Clark National Park, since it is accessible only by floatplane. Your private guide for the day will pilot your seaplane from Anchorage over cascading glacial icefields and wide valleys dotted with browsing moose. You will land at choice spots along the way to picnic and fish for grayling and lake trout, coming at last to Lake Iliamna with its trophy salmon and rainbow trout. Your trip includes fishing license, all gear and a private pilot/guide. Your flight home over glaciers, wildlife and the Cook Inlet oil platforms tops off this very personalized day of trophy fishing. **June-Sept.**

Alaska Wilderness Travel. 121 W. Fireweed, Anchorage, AK 99503. (907) 277-7671, 1-800-544-2236.

Aniakchak
National Monument and Preserve

The central feature of the Aniakchak National Monument and Preserve is the volcanic Aniakchak Caldera created by the collapse of the central part of a volcano sometime after the last glaciation age. The caldera covers 48 square kilometers (30 square miles) and is 9.7 kilometers (6 miles) wide. Later activity built a cone, Vent Mountain, inside the caldera. Aniakchak last erupted in 1931. The caldera's Surprise Lake, heated by hot springs, cascades through a 460-meter (1,500-foot) rift in the crater wall. Such volcanic features as lava floes, cinder cones, and explosion pits can be seen here, along with hardy pioneer plant communities etching life into an Aleutian moonscape.

Wildlife on the 586,000 acres of monument and preserve includes occasional caribou, grizzly bear and eagles. Sockeye salmon spawn in the Aniakchak River, which originates in Surprise Lake. Fish from this watershed are recognizable by the flavor of soda and iron characteristic of the caldera's mineral-laden outflow.

Aniakchak is one of the most remote national park areas, and weather on the Alaska Peninsula can be stormy at all seasons. Scheduled airline service to King Salmon can put you within moderate charter flight distance of the preserve. Floatplanes can land on Surprise Lake.

Information: Superintendent, Aniakchak National Monument and Preserve, PO Box 7, King Salmon, AK 99613. (907) 271-4243.

Overlooking the volcanic Aniakchak Caldera. (NPS photo)

PAINTER CREEK LODGE

Located in the heart of Alaska's renowned Bristol Bay fishery, the Painter Creek area offers some of the world's best sportfishing. Although fishing is a primary attraction, there are also many other opportunities for outdoor adventure. Situated in the remote reaches of the Alaska Peninsula, Painter Creek Lodge is surrounded by the Alaska Peninsula National Wildlife Refuge and Aniakchak National Park and Preserve. This pristine wilderness area abounds in wildlife, including brown bear, moose, caribou, wolverine, lynx, and a variety of smaller animals. It is also a nesting and staging area for millions of waterfowl and other bird species. One may choose to spend time observing the area's unique geological features, including active volcanoes, or hike, beachcomb, photograph or raft. **June-Oct.**

Painter Creek Lodge. Box 1350, Palmer, AK 99645. (907) 745-3772.

Bud Rice

ANIAKCHAK VOLCANO HIKE/RAFT

This extremely remote mountainous setting features the Aniakchak caldera, a giant, inactive collapsed volcano. Vast fields of ash, cinder, and lava deposits are slowly being carpeted by alpine vegetation. You'll fly into Surprise Lake, which is fed by warm springs, and spend 2-5 days hiking from a base camp around the caldera. Next you take a challenging whitewater run out of Caldera Lake down the Aniakchak River, part of the National Wild and Scenic River System. The river runs through the central portion of the Alaska Peninsula Wildlife Refuge which contains an extremely productive fish population of salmon and trout, and is also a prime habitat for caribou, moose, fox, wolf, bear, wolverine, and waterfowl. The weather is commonly windy, wet and cloudy. This remote, rugged wilderness area is one of the most forbidding yet fascinating places in Alaska. **Sept.**

Alaska Treks N Voyages. PO Box 600-K, Moose Pass, AK 99631. (907) 288-3610 or 224-3960.

The Aleutian Invasion

Japan's brief incursion into the Aleutian Islands during World War II was the first invasion of American soil since 1812. After losing over 3,000 troops in fierce fighting on Attu the Japanese recognized that the venture was a miscalculation and abruptly abandoned it. The Aleutian invasion was kept secret from the American public first in the name of preserving civilian morale and later to avoid embarrassing the military for blunders committed here.

Subsequent efforts to clean up war debris have floundered because of the great distances involved and incessantly inclement weather. Clean-up efforts at this late date may cause as much environmental harm as good. Since the Park Service has vetoed designating battlegrounds here as historic sites, it appears that only the extensive fortifications and debris will remain as memorials to the thousands of soldiers who lost their lives on these cloudy, wind swept islands.

Bob Gilmore photo/FWS

Southwest

Alaska Peninsula
National Wildlife Refuge

The Alaska Peninsula Refuge is dominated by the rugged Aleutian Range, part of an area along the Pacific Ocean, known as the "ring of fire," which is particularly susceptible to volcanic activity. Of the 60 volcanoes in the Aleutian Range, 25 are on the Alaska Peninsula.

Large mammals found on the refuge include brown bear, wolves, and wolverines. Almost 3,000 bears roam the peninsula south of Becharof Lake creating the world's densest bear population. A few hundred years ago moose weren't found here, but recently they have migrated down the peninsula from the mainland as far as Port Moller. Large populations of Steller sea lions, harbor seals, sea otters and migratory whales inhabit the coastal waters. The population of sea otters on the Pacific side of the peninsula numbers at least 30,000--in contrast to the 1880's when they were nearly extinct.

Waterfowl dependent on the refuge include nesting whistling swans, emperor geese, migrating Canada geese and 25 species of ducks. Cormorants, murres, puffins, kittiwakes, gulls, terns, jaegers and murrelets are the marine bird species that nest on Pacific cliffs. Murrelets, especially the Kittlitz's species, prefer to nest in seclusion and fly inland great distances to make their nest sites. Bald eagles and peregrine falcons nest on coastal cliffs.

The Alaska Peninsula Refuge is renowned for big game hunting, especially for moose, caribou and brown bear. Fishing is outstanding for king and silver salmon, arctic char, lake trout, dolly varden, northern pike, and grayling. Five pound char and grayling are common trophies from the Ugashik Lakes. In 1981, the world's record grayling was caught on the refuge. Kayaking the coastal bays and inlets affords wildlife viewing opportunities.

Information: Refuge Manager, Alaska Peninsula National Wildlife Refuge, PO Box 277, King Salmon, AK 99613. (907) 246-3339.

Bull sea lion and harem (John Fowler photo)

Izembek
National Wildlife Refuge

Izembek faces the Bering Sea on the tip of the Alaska Peninsula. The landscape includes volcanos with glacier caps, valleys, and tundra uplands that slope into lagoons adjoining the Bering Sea.

Izembek Lagoon contains the world's largest eelgrass beds and is one of the first four U.S. wetlands to receive international recognition. These beds are part of a large estuary that provides a haven for migratory birds. The world's entire population of black brant (a small coastal goose), many thousands of Canada and emperor geese and other waterfowl congregate on the lagoon to feed on the eelgrass.

Most waterfowl arrive on the refuge in late August or early September. By October, over one million birds have taken up residence on the refuge. By early November a second wave of northern waterfowl (primarily sea ducks) arrive to winter on Izembek. The colorful Steller's eider (which nests on the arctic coast of Alaska and Siberia) is the most common wintering duck in the lagoon. In addition, thousands of shore birds feed at low tide on the bay's invertebrates. At high tide they gather in such large flocks that in flight they appear as dense smoke clouds. In the tundra uplands, Savannah sparrows, peregrine falcons, bald eagles and whistling swans are year-round residents. Gyrfalcons and golden eagles are also known to breed here. One of Alaska's most undisturbed populations of brown bear roams the refuge. In the summer the bears feed on runs of red, silver and chum salmon that spawn in local streams. Other wildlife includes wolves, barren-ground caribou and ptarmigan. Several thousand hair seals haul out on the sand spits of the refuge and nearby waters hold sea lion, three types of seals, porpoises, walrus and beluga whales. Historically, the waters of Izembek Lagoon may have been home to the Steller's sea cow, a now-extinct relative of the manatee that reached lengths of 26 feet and weighed two tons.

Izembek has outstanding waterfowl hunting; ptarmigan are also often hunted. Caribou hunting is excellent. Fine opportunities exist for bird watching and photography, salmon and trout fishing, canoeing and kayaking, hiking the upland valleys and observing wildlife. There are some roads (trails) to the refuge from Cold Bay but most of the refuge is accessible only by boat or foot. Izembek is cloudy, foggy and incessantly windy. The area has the lowest recorded rate of solar radiation received anywhere in North America.

Information: Refuge Manager, Izembek National Wildlife Refuge, Pouch 2, Cold Bay, AK 99571. (907) 532-2445.

Waterfowl rising from Izembek Lagoon (FWS photo)

Alaska Maritime
National Wildlife Refuge

The Alaska Maritime refuge is an aggregation of more than 2,400 islands, headlands, rocks, islets, spires and reefs along various portions of the Alaskan coast. The refuge is divided into five geographical units.

The Chukchi Sea includes Capes Lisburne and Thompson which together protect the largest colonial seabird nesting sites along Alaska's arctic coast.

To the south, the Bering Sea unit includes St Matthew Island, Hall Island, and the Pribilof and Pinnacle islands. The latter islands include a five-mile-long rookery containing the world's largest fulmar colony. The tundra highlands of St. Matthew Island are the only known nesting area for the rare McKay's snow bunting. The Pribilof Islands are home to a million fur seals --the largest gathering of wild mammals anywhere on earth. Pribilof cliffs are home to the largest known breeding population of red-faced cormorants and one of only two known red-legged kittewake breeding locations.

The Aleutian Islands unit consists of islands and shorelines of the Aleutian Chain as well as 2.7 million acres on Unimak Island. The refuge boasts a sea otter population in the tens of thousands. The rare Kittilitz's murrelet nests here, as well as the Aleutian Canada goose and the rare (if not extinct) short-tailed albatross. Dozens of Asian birds are recorded here (especially on Attu) that can be seen nowhere else in North America.

The Shumagik Island archipelago, Simeonof Island, the Semidi Islands and the Murie Islets comprise the refuge's Alaska Peninsula Unit. It has been set aside primarily to protect sea otter habitat and is the only Alaskan refuge to include offshore waters as part of its protected acreage. Rare marine bird species that nest here include rhinoceros auklets and marbled and Kittilitz's murrelets.

Tuxedni Island in Cook Inlet, the Barren Islands in the Gulf of Alaska, St. Lazaria Island, Forrester Island and the Hazy Island in Southeastern Alaska are the major protected areas of the Gulf of Alaska unit of the refuge. Alaska's largest sea lion rookery is protected on Sugarloaf Island.

Information: Refuge Manager, Alaska Maritime National Wildlife Refuge, 202 Pioneer Avenue, Homer, AK 99603. (907) 235-6546. Aleutian Islands contact: Alaska Maritime National Wildlife Refuge, Aleutian Islands Unit, Box 5251, FPO Seattle, WA 98791. (907) 592-2406.

Pribilof fur seals (Brett Coburn photo/ St. George Tanaq Corp.)

Brett Coburn

ST. GEORGE, PRIBILOF ISLANDS

Often referred to as the Galapagos of the North, the Pribilof Islands are known worldwide for their exotic array of wildlife--including nearly one million fur seals (80% of the world's fur seal population), and over 200 species of seabirds which migrate by the millions to the islands each summer. Upon arrival at St. George, you will find a volcanic island bordered by precipitous cliffs, the highest of which rises well over a thousand feet from the rocky shoreline below. The secluded village of St. George, with its fascinating Aleut-Russian history, is surrounded by lush fields of treeless tundra covered in summer with wildflowers. A visit to St. George Island will be of special interest to the wildlife enthusiast.
June-Sept.

St. George Tanaq Corporation. 2604 Fairbanks St., Anchorage, AK 99503. (907) 276-3600.

David Grimes photo

Volcanos

One tenth of the world's volcanos are found in Alaska. The southern coast is part of the "Rim of Fire," an arc of volcanically active zones bordering the Pacific. The susceptibility to volcanic activity in these zones results from the collision of the Pacific plate of the earth's crust and surrounding continental plates. Since the 1700's, 40 of the state's 89 volcanos have experienced major eruptions. One of the world's most violent eruptions occurred here in 1912 when Novarupta (now part of Katmai National Park) blew 40 times more earth than was excavated from the Panama Canal as high as 50,000 feet into the atmosphere. Mt. Pavlov, located northeast of Cold Bay, is North America's most active volcano having erupted 26 time since the 1700's. Bogoslof Island, located 35 miles northwest of Dutch Harbor, boiled out of the Bering Sea on May 18, 1796 and has since disappeared and reformed more than once.

Volcanic activity in the Chigmit Mountain area is relatively frequent and easily visible from Anchorage and the Kenai Peninsula. The Wrangell Mountains include some of the world's highest volcanos, including Mt. Blackburn (16,390 ft.), Mt. Sanford (16,237 ft.) and active Mt. Wrangell (14,163 ft.). Recent studies have found that most of Alaska is composed of volcanic islands and seamounts (like Hawaii) which have moved north on the Pacific plate over millions of years (at an average rate of two inches per year) and then been scraped off and flattened against North America as the Pacific plate has forced its way beneath the lighter continental plate.

Southeast

Southeast Alaska is stretched along 500 miles of very rugged and beautiful wilderness coastline running from the towering St. Elias Mountains on the north to the Dixon Entrance and Hecate Strait on the south. The Alexander Archipelago, a spectacular group of over 1,000 islands, lie clustered along this coast. The Tongass National Forest, the nation's largest protected forest, encompasses nearly the entire area.

Southeast is a land of water in all its forms. Moisture laden air moving in off the Pacific sheds as much as 200 inches of rain on the more exposed coastal lowlands. Precipitation falling in the coastal mountains can produce 400 to 600 inches of snowfall per year. Rain and meltwater from mountain ice fields nurture the area's dense maritime forests. Rivers of ice, snow and crushed rock flow down through broad valleys and break crashing into the sea. The protected salt waters of the Inside Passage provide ideal habitat for humpback whale, orca, porpoise, and seal. Winters here are mild and summers generally cool.

Southeast is connected to a road system running from Prince Rupert south through British Columbia. On the north, roads run from Skagway and Haines through the Yukon Territory and into Alaska's Interior. However, travel within Southeast itself is possible only by boat or plane. Taking a state ferry or a cruise ship through Southeast as the beginning or final leg of a trip to Alaska is very popular and highly recommended.

Because of the region's spectacular geography and remoteness, the towns of Southeast are unusually picturesque. Juneau, the state's capitol, is located here. Sitka and Skagway are both sites of national historic parks. Glacier Bay National Park, Admiralty Island National Monument and Misty Fjords National Monument are the wilderness centerpieces of this striking region.

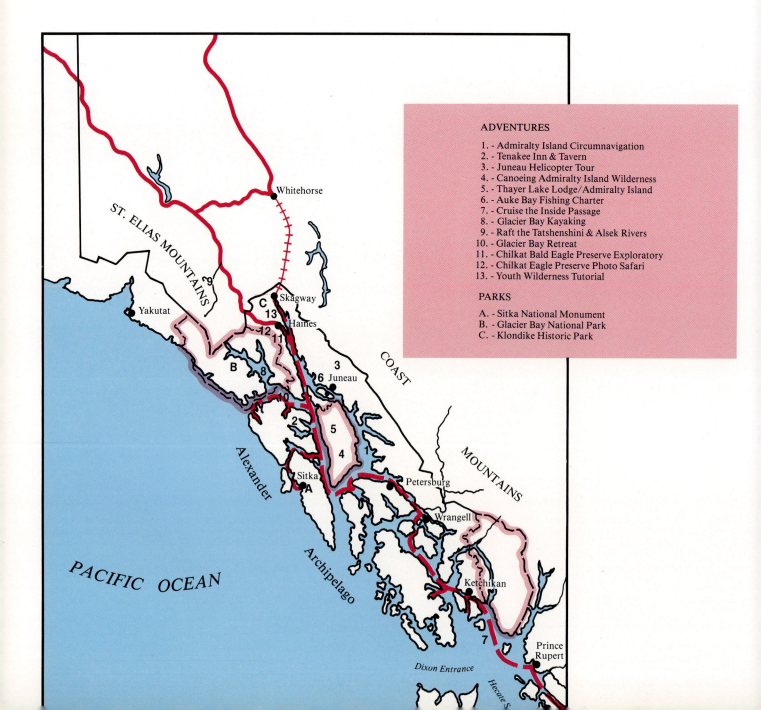

ADVENTURES

1. - Admiralty Island Circumnavigation
2. - Tenakee Inn & Tavern
3. - Juneau Helicopter Tour
4. - Canoeing Admiralty Island Wilderness
5. - Thayer Lake Lodge/Admiralty Island
6. - Auke Bay Fishing Charter
7. - Cruise the Inside Passage
8. - Glacier Bay Kayaking
9. - Raft the Tatshenshini & Alsek Rivers
10. - Glacier Bay Retreat
11. - Chilkat Bald Eagle Preserve Exploratory
12. - Chilkat Eagle Preserve Photo Safari
13. - Youth Wilderness Tutorial

PARKS

A. - Sitka National Monument
B. - Glacier Bay National Park
C. - Klondike Historic Park

Chilkat Lake and Four Winds Mountain from Takhin Ridge (Al Gilliam photo/Alaska Cross Country Guiding and Rafting)

State Ferry System
Southeast

The Alaska State Ferry provides the only regularly-scheduled surface passenger and freight service through Southeast Alaska. Ferries run from Seattle and Prince Rupert through the "Inside Passage" and connect with road systems at Skagway and Haines to the Yukon Territory and Interior Alaska. The ferry trip from Seattle along the coast of British Columbia to the logging and fishing community of Ketchikan at the southern tip of Alaska's "Panhandle" takes just under two days (41 hours). The ferry continues north through the Alexander Archipelago to the logging town of Wrangell (known for its Tlingit Indian petroglyphs), then to the fishing village of Petersburg which was first settled by Scandinavian immigrants. The ferry also stops at Juneau, Alaska's capital, before going on to Skagway and Haines. Total trip time from Ketchikan to Haines is about a day and a half.

Special ferry routes also serve the smaller towns of Metlakatla, Hollis, Kake, Sitka, Pelican, Hoonah, Angoon and Tenakee Springs. Commercially-operated tours and facilities are available in some of these communities. There is no charge for stopovers if booked in advance. Scheduled jet airliners serve Ketchikan, Wrangell, Petersburg, Sitka and Juneau.

State ferries are informal and comfortable. Walk-on passengers can bring hand luggage and coin-operated lockers are available. Staterooms which accommodate one to four persons are available on longer routes. Reservations are required for vehicles, staterooms and, on some routes, for walk-on passengers. However, standbys are taken on a space available basis. One-way fare for passengers from Prince Rupert to **Haines is about $90 and $227 for a 15-foot vehicle**.

Information: Alaska Marine Highway, PO Box R, Juneau, AK 99811. 1-800-642-0066; Juneau (907) 456-3941; Anchorage (907) 272-7116; Seattle (206) 632-1970.

Alaska ferry docked in Haines (Nancy Simmerman photo/ AlaskaPhoto)

Sitka
National Historical Park

Sitka is one of Alaska's most picturesque and historically significant cities. Sitka National Historical Park covers 108 acres and preserves the site of the 1804 fort and battle that marked the last major resistance of the Tlingit Indians to Russian colonization. This was Russian-America's political, economic and cultural capital for half a century. The park includes a collection of Tlingit totems and its visitor center exhibits and explains Pacific Northwest Coast Indian art.

Well before the Russian explorers reached this shore, the Tlingit followed the salmon streams southward to settle here at "Shee Atika." The Tlingit enjoyed a rich, highly developed culture and military superiority over most neighboring tribes. This preeminence was challenged by the Russian-American Company's colonization under the leadership of Alexander Baranov. Although Baranov obtained permission to establish a post near the Tlingit fort of Shee Atika, the Tlingit subsequently changed their minds about the venture and massacred the settlers. Baranov, in turn, succeeded in driving the Tlingit into the forests, burned their fort, and built the new town of New Archangel (now Sitka).

Sitka is served by state-operated ferries, commercial cruiseships, and daily jet service.

Information: Superintendent, Sitka National Historical Park, PO Box 738, Sitka, AK 99835. (907) 271-4243.

Haida totem of Tlingit legend, Lakich-inei and child, on park trail (Cathy Hart photo)

Southeast

Juneau

Juneau, the state capital, is the most frequently visited city in Southeast. With 22,000 residents, it is also the largest city in the region and a supply center for the surrounding area. Seattle is only two hours and 25 minutes by air and Anchorage only an hour and a quarter. Regular commercial flights out of Juneau also serve Ketchikan, Wrangell, Petersburg, Sitka, Gustavus and Yakutat and local air taxis and ocean charters offer scheduled and unscheduled service to smaller towns. Juneau is a popular layover for visitors arriving on cruise ships or the state ferry.

Although Auke Bay Tlingit Indians hunted and foraged at the site of present day Juneau, it wasn't until 1880 when Chief Kowee told Joe Juneau and Richard Harris about the rich gold veins here that the area became permanently settled. In the rush that followed, Juneau became one of the most productive gold mining areas in the world. Today the miner's homes tucked against the mountains, wooden stairs climbing the slopes and abandoned mine shafts remain as legacies of this era.

Downtown Juneau is a very pleasant mix of modern and turn-of-the-century architecture, including a massive and striking cement government office building, an antebellum governor's mansion, a Russian Orthodox church and many beautifully preserved slat board homes and commercial buildings.

Juneau is nestled against the base of Mt. Juneau which towers above the Gastineau Channel like a green-clad giant cooling its toes in the ocean. The impressive Mendenhall Glacier flows out of the 1,500 square mile Juneau Ice Field just 20 minutes from downtown. Numerous trails run through the towering spruce and hemlock forests and up to dramatic mountain vistas which overlook the surrounding waterways.

Information: Juneau Visitor Information Center. 134 Third Street, Juneau, AK 99801. (907) 586-2201 or 586-2284.

Cruise ship overnighting at Juneau (DOT photo)

ACVB photo

Cathy Hart

ADMIRALTY ISLAND CIRCUMNAVIGATION

This five-to-seven day 300-mile ocean charter takes you to fjords, ice fields, active glaciers, brown bear, fishing salmon-choked streams, eagles, humpback whales, porpoises, seals and sea lions. Departing from Juneau, you will join a small group for a safe, comfortable, experience packed wilderness cruise. You'll visit a hot springs, a fish hatchery, an Indian village, and Tenakee, a remote town that time has barely changed. In secluded overnight anchorages, the sweet forest air and the tang of the salt air blend in an intoxicating aroma. You and your companions are likely to be the only people for many miles. Exploring historic ruins, fishing, crabbing and beach combing are some of the in-cruise options. Be a spectator or a participant. Scheduled cruises and custom charters are available. **May-Sept.**

Alaska Sea Adventures. 318 Coleman Dr., Juneau, Alaska 99801. (907) 586-1947, 1-800-252-7527.

TENAKEE INN AND TAVERN

Weekly ferry runs or a small plane charter from Juneau bring you to the Tenakee Inn overlooking Tenakee Inlet. The Inn provides a taste of architectural history in the wilderness and a range of recreational choices. A 31-foot Uniflight charter is available for salmon and halibut fishing as well as whalewatching excursions. You can explore the sheltered inlets on your own via kayak or skiff, scan the shores for wildlife or make a short portage to visit the Indian village of Hoonah. Chichagof Island and its waters are home to deer, bear, mink, otter, martin, porpoise, sea lion, seal, whale, and eagle. Bicyclers and hikers can take advantage of numerous trails across the island. Upon your return to the inn you can rest as you whalewatch on the balcony or relax in Tenakee's hot springs. Kayak, skiff and bicycle rentals available. **June-Dec.**

Alaska Wilderness Travel. 121 W. Fireweed, Anchorage, AK 99503. (907) 277-7671, 1-800-544-2236.

JUNEAU HELICOPTER TOUR

Tucked in along the base of 3,600-foot Mt. Juneau, Alaska's capital city sits on the continent side of the Gastineau channel. Your aerial tour will allow you an extraordinary perspective of the Juneau Ice Field, a 1,500-square mile ice field descending from the Coast Mountains. You'll continue on to a 12-mile river of ice known as the Mendenhall Glacier. At its terminus you can observe huge sections of ice calving off to become icebergs in Mendenhall Lake. Your pilot will land on a glacier for 15 minutes of close-up viewing. On your return flight, watch the flanks of the snow-capped Chilkoot Range for mountain goats. Tour time is 65 minutes. **Year-round.**

Alaska Wilderness Travel. 121 W. Fireweed, Anchorage, AK 99503. (907) 277-7671, 1-800-544-2236.

CANOEING ADMIRALTY ISLAND WILDERNESS

Admiralty Island, called Kootznahoo or "Fortress of the Bears," by the Tlingit Indians who have lived here thousands of years, has its own system of lakes and a network of trails. To the west lies the Indian village of Angoon. Towering spruce forests grow atop rich, moss-carpeted soils, providing food and shelter to some of the largest concentrations of both bald eagles and brown bear in the world. Your 5 or 7-day trip leaves by charter flight from Juneau. On the 7-day float you traverse 7 tranquil lakes, fishing freshwater for cutthroat trout and the ocean for salmon. On the 5-day wildlife safari you observe bear, eagle, deer, seal, sea lion, and whale. The fishing is excellent as you canoe protected saltwaters from one salmon stream estuary to the next, camping beneath spruce and hemlock canopies. **May-Sept.**

Alaska Wilderness Travel. 121 W. Fireweed, Anchorage, AK 99503. (907) 277-7671, 1-800-544-2236.

THAYER LAKE LODGE / ADMIRALTY ISLAND

Thayer Lake Lodge is a family-built wilderness resort, continuously operated by the Nelsons since 1947. The lodge is situated in the heart of Admiralty Island National Monument, a roadless area of approximately one million acres, accessible only by plane and trail. This nook in the wilderness offers guests the opportunity of stepping off a trail and being where no one has set foot before. The lodge offers trout fishing, hiking, a river float trip and tidal exploration, canoeing, and the chance to fish the Angoon/Killisnoo salmon grounds. Only sixty air miles from Juneau, the lodge has all modern facilities and offers a choice of American Plan accommodations with family style meals or housekeeping cabins for your privacy. All package trips include round trip transportation from Juneau. **April-Sept.**

Thayer Lake Lodge. PO Box 5416, Ketchikan, AK 99901. (907) 225-3343 or 789-0944.

AUKE BAY FISHING CHARTER

This adventure begins in historic Auke Bay, an early Tlingit Indian village site just north of Juneau. Free van service will deliver you to dockside where you'll board your comfortable, fully-equipped charter vessel. Coast Guard licensed Captain, Ken Wicks, is a long-time Alaskan with 15 years experience boating and fishing in Southeast Alaska. Daily charters range from half-day to full-day excursions. Special charters are available for overnight trips to Glacier Bay National Park, Tenakee Hot Springs, Gustavis, and the Tlingit Indian village of Hoonah. These Southeast ports are 4 to 8 hours from Juneau, each offering its own unique and fascinating attractions. **June-Nov.**

Alaska Wilderness Travel. 121 W. Fireweed, Anchorage, AK 99503. (907) 277-7671, 1-800-544-2236.

Mark Kelley

John Fowler

CRUISING THE INSIDE PASSAGE

Luxury liners offer an elegant, comfortable and relaxing way to explore Alaska. Cruising through the calm waters of the Inside Passage you will pass countless forested islands, deep fjords, cascading waterfalls, towering snowcapped peaks, and massive glaciers. Whale, porpoise, seal, eagle and bear may be viewed from the deck or from the comfort of the lounge. Shoreside excursions include trips to colorful fishing and logging communities and historic towns, including Ketchikan, Sitka, Juneau, Skagway, Haines, Valdez, Homer, Seward and Anchorage. Chefs provide fine gourmet cooking, often featuring Alaskan king crab, salmon, and halibut. On-board activities include everything from exercise classes to professional entertainment. Cruise ships depart from Los Angeles, San Francisco, Seattle, Vancouver and Prince Rupert. **June-Sept.**

Alaska Wilderness Travel. 121 W. Fireweed, Anchorage, AK 99503. (907) 277-7671, 1-800-544-2236.

Cathy Hart

Glaciers

Alaska's spectacular concentrations of glaciers are not the result of a frigid climate. The coldest parts of the state have the fewest glaciers. Glaciers form over long periods of time where snow accumulation exceeds melting. Alaska's coastal mountains (the world's highest coastal mountains) catch heavy snowfall formed from moist Pacific air masses. At the altitude where snow accumulates faster than it melts, the snow compresses under its own weight into dense blue ice which will flow downhill (at an imperceptibly slow rate) under the influence of gravity.

These vast rivers of ice push up massive mounds of crushed rock (moraines) and scoop out broad valleys. As with a river, the topography of a glacier's surface is a function of its rate of flow and the roughness of the surface beneath it. A glacier surface with numerous cracks and crevasses is indicative of an uneven rock bed. The grinding of ice flowing over bedrock produces fine rock powder or "glacial flour" which colors many of Alaska's rivers a distinctive gray and provides mineral nutrients to soils.

The Chugach Mountains in Southcentral Alaska hold the highest concentration of glaciers in the state. The Bering Glacier, part of the Chugach's Bagley Icefield, is North America's largest glacier and at 100 miles is also its longest. The Black Rapids Glacier in the Alaska Range gained the name "galloping glacier" for its six-mile advance in six months in 1936-37, sometimes gaining 115 feet per day.

Southeast

Glacier Bay
National Park and Preserve

Glacier Bay National Park and Preserve contains some of the world's most impressive examples of tidewater glaciers, with some 16 active glaciers in all. The bay has experienced at least four major advances and four major retreats of glaciation and serves as an outdoor laboratory for contemporary research. Mountains here rise almost 5 vertical kilometers (3 miles) from tidewater, making them among the world's highest in terms of vertical rise. A diverse variety of plant communities ranges from terrain just recovering from glacial retreat to lush temperate rain forest. Nowhere is the story of plant succession more dramatically illustrated than here at Glacier Bay.

The 3.28 million acres of the park and preserve host brown and black bear, whale and seal, as well as eagle and over 200 other species of birds. The park's Mount Fairweather (15,300 feet) is the highest peak in southeastern Alaska.

Glacier Bay is accessible by commercial cruiseship, charter boat, or aircraft, or by scheduled air and boat service from Juneau and other southeastern Alaska communities.

Information: Superintendent, Glacier Bay National Park and Preserve, Box 1089, Juneau, AK 99802 or Bartlett Cove, Gustavus, AK 99826. (907) 271-4243.

Tidewater glacier in the park (Rob Bosworth photo/ Alaska Discovery)

Hayden Kayden

Kevin Cassity

GLACIER BAY KAYAKING

No previous boating experience is necessary to enjoy the backcountry of Glacier Bay National Park by touring kayak. Seals and porpoises will be your companions as you paddle into the heart of this mountain and ocean wilderness. Humpback and orca whale, brown and black bear, coyote, wolf, and mountain goat are among the many types of wildlife you may spot. The cliffs and beaches are home to bald eagle and such exotic bird species as puffin, guillemot, murrelet, oystercatcher, and many others. Itineraries are flexible on these four to seven day trips, allowing ample time for photography, beachcombing, and short hikes as you kayak from one pristine campsite to the next. Finally, a bush floatplane takes you back over the fjords you've paddled, past the 15,000 foot Fairweather Range, then to Juneau. **June-Sept.**

Alaska Discovery. PO Box 021892-A, Juneau, AK 99801. (907) 586-1911.

RAFT THE TATSHENSHINI & ALSEK RIVERS

Known to river runners across the country, the 10-day Tatshenshini-Alsek float is one of the world's premier wilderness raft trips. You depart from Haines, at the northern tip of the Inside Passage, and drive through 100 miles of scenic wilderness into Canada to the river's edge in the lush green hills of historic Dalton Post. Unnamed tributaries carve immense valleys which disappear into white, crystalline mountains. The St. Elias Range rises above you, eagles glide overhead, and around each bend you look for passing bear, moose, or the furtive wolf. As you enter the Alsek River several glaciers border the river banks. Your destination is Dry Bay on the Gulf of Alaska where charter planes wait to fly you along the Outside Coast to Yakatat for connecting scheduled air service. **July-Sept.**

Alaska Wilderness Co-op. 4341 MacAlister Dr., Anchorage, AK 99515. (907) 243-3068.

GLACIER BAY RETREAT

Just three miles from Glacier Bay National Park, nestled into a forested countryside sits a cozy inn. At less than a half hour by air from Juneau, life at the inn will make you feel a world away from the rush of modern life. You will enjoy relaxing around the homestead, hiking in the dense rain forest, berry picking, bird watching and fishing in nearby Icy Straits for salmon and halibut. And, of course, there's Glacier Bay where you can enjoy naturalist-led walks, boat cruises (both day and overnight trips), flightseeing tours and kayak trips. Your hosts provide warm, personal attention, and meals at the inn feature homebaked breads, garden-fresh produce and local seafoods. **Year Round.**

Alaska Wilderness Travel. 121 W. Fireweed, Anchorage, AK 99503. (907) 277-7671, 1-800-544-2236.

Southeast

Klondike
National Historical Park

When an 1897 issue of the Seattle Post-Intelligencer reported that a steamer from Alaska had put in at Seattle with a ton of gold aboard, it touched off the last of the great gold rushes. At the height of the rush John Muir called Skagway "a nest of ants taken into a strange country and stirred up by a stick." Klondike Gold Rush National Historical Park preserves historic Skagway buildings from this period as well as portions of the Chilkoot and White Pass Trails into the Klondike.

The park's 13,270 acres offer a variety of experiences, in both small town and wilderness settings. A lively turn-of-the-century flavored nightlife thrives in Skagway, a regular port of call for cruiseships. Skagway is also the southern end of Alaska's first railroad which ran over the White Pass to Whitehorse. The Trail of '98 Museum is housed here in Alaska's first granite building. Backpacking over the Chilkoot and White passes has also become increasingly popular.

Visitors can reach the park by ferry, cruiseship, railroad, commuter airline, air taxi, or by car.

Information: Superintendent, Klondike Gold Rush National Historical Park, PO Box 517, Skagway, AK 99840. (907) 271-4243.

Gold rush era entertainment (John Fowler photo)

John Fowler

CHILKAT BALD EAGLE PRESERVE EXPLORATORY

This very personalized adventure vacation for two begins near the town of Haines, which is the terminus for the Alaska Ferry System and the beginning of the highway to interior Alaska. Guide Al Gilliam, a 12-year resident of Haines, will welcome you to his 1931 log cabin homestead with a spectacular slide show of the entire back country. The three of you will plan your 10-day excursion to include a combination of floating or canoeing through the preserve, air boating into the backcountry, hiking beautiful and remote reaches of the dramatic upper valleys and alpine valleys, and fishing for trout and salmon. The scenery ranges from moss-laden rain forests to dry lodge-pole pine country to raw, primitive glacier lands. Your wilderness guide's skills include photography, big game calling, woodsmanship, wildlife lore and natural history. **May-Dec.**

Alaska Cross Country Guiding and Rafting. Box 124, Haines, Alaska 99827.

CHILKAT EAGLE PRESERVE PHOTO SAFARI

During late summer and early fall, when the rivers are thick with salmon and the autumn colors are at their finest, your wilderness guide will lead 1 or 2 guests on an exclusive 10-day photo safari. This is the time of year when the eagle population of the Chilkat drainage begins to swell to about 4,000. In such remote and picturesque areas as the Takhin Valley, eagles share the habitat with bear, wolf, wolverine, and otter. Pre-recorded animal distress sounds, strategically placed scents and wildlife blinds are used to entice animals within camera range. The lighting conditions and more moderate temperatures of this season create excellent photographic opportunities. The safari takes you through some of the most magnificent, rugged country in Southeast. **Aug-Dec.**

Alaska Wilderness Co-op. 4341 MacAlister Drive, Anchorage, AK 99515. (907) 243-3068.

YOUTH WILDERNESS TUTORIAL

The Chilkat Bald Eagle Preserve, 49,000 acres of spectacular, primitive country, will be the site of this tutorial for the young adventurer. This introduction to the wilderness is for those age 14 and up. The instructor will work closely with one or two students to allow close communication and to insure a rewarding experience. River rafting, canoeing, hiking and survival skills will be taught. Animal lore is discussed at length while exploring areas where Alaskan wildlife can be observed in undisturbed settings. Fishing is excellent for salmon and trout. Information on proper outdoor clothing, nutrition, philosophy and technique will be shared throughout the course. **May-Sept.**

Alaska Wilderness Travel. 121 W. Fireweed, Anchorage, AK 99503. (907) 277-7671, 1-800-544-2236.

John Fowler photo

THE ALASKA TRAVEL PAGES™

Limited Edition
Wildlife Prints

by John Fowler

Limited edition prints available at Graphic Art Plus in Anchorage at the Dimond, Northway and University malls and in Fairbanks at the Bentley Mall.

John Fowler, Box 670696
Chugiak, Alaska 99567
(907) 272-8733

Accommodations

Alaskans are often far from family and hometown friends and are some of the most hospitable people you'll meet. So if an Alaskan ever says, "Stay with us when you some to Alaska," chances are the invitation is sincere. Phone first, though, as Alaskans are often on the move.

There is a full range of hotels and motels in Alaska's larger cities, ranging from $25 a night ("working person's") to $500 for the most luxurious suites. Most rooms cost $100 to $150/night in summer, $75 to $125 in winter. Rates are generally comparable in smaller communities.

Bed and breakfast inns are a good way to meet Alaskans and get tips about the country over good home cooking. Prices start at $25 a night per person.

RV travel is a great way to see the outdoors, but facilities are usually simple; don't expect luxury campgrounds. For more information see "Auto/RV Rentals."

Campgrounds maintained by the U. S. Bureau of Land Management are still free but expect fees of $3 to $10 per night on some public lands (higher in private facilities). "Walk in" tent campsites are available in many parks. Cabins in National Forests and on Bureau of Land Management property may be rented for $10 a night by prearrangement. Three-sided shelters are usually free. Most are reached by hiking. Location maps are available through the BLM. For more information see "Parks and Public Lands."

Some wilderness lodges are accessible by road but many can be reached only by air. Facilities range from primitive, with rustic cabins and pit toilets, to luxurious fly-in hunting and fishing lodges with gourmet cooking at $2,000 or more per week. For further information see "Lodges/Rustic Cabins."

Anchorage

Alaska Private Lodgings. (See advertisement this page). 1236 W. 10th Avenue, Anchorage, AK 99501. (907) 258-1717.

Alaska Wilderness Travel. (See adventure pgs. 17, 97, & 101) 121 W. Fireweed, Anchorage, AK 99503. (907) 277-7671, 1-800-544-2236.

Alaska's Tudor Motel. (See advertisement this page). 4423 Lake Otis Parkway, Anchorage, AK 99507. (907) 561-2234.

Inlet Towers Hotel. (See advertisement this page). Home away from home. Six blocks from downtown. Airport shuttle. Complimentary coffee. Saunas, exercise equipment, satellite TV, laundry facilities. Free parking. 1200 L Street, Anchorage, AK 99501. (907) 276-0110. Toll free (800) 544-0786.

Haines

Captain's Choice Motel. (See advertisement this page). Ultra-modern accommodations with TV, HBO, coffee or tea, telephone, bath & shower in each room. Some kitchenettes. Executive suite boasts wet bar and private patio. Panoramic view of Portage Cove, Lynn Canal and boat harbor. Walking distance to everything. Year-round service. Eagle watchers and fishing packages available. $55-$100. Brochure. VS, MC, AE, DC, CB. Write: Box 392, Haines, AK 99827. (907) 766-2461.

Bed & Breakfast

Accommodations in private homes, downtown to wilderness, Anchorage, Willow, Talkeetna, Healy, Homer and Soldotna. A great way to see Alaska!

ALASKA PRIVATE LODGINGS
For reservations and information:
1236 W. 10th Ave.
Anchorage, Alaska 99501   (907) 258-1717

The All-Suite Experience

Anchorage's Inlet Towers Hotel

Spacious suites with complete kitchens, quiet comfort and a spectacular view...all for the price of an ordinary hotel room.

Six blocks from downtown
Airport shuttle · Complimentary coffee
Saunas · Exercise Equipment
Satellite TV · Laundry facilities
Free parking
1200 L Street, Anchorage, Alaska 99501

(907) 276-0110
toll free from Western states
800-544-0786
or book through SABRE (31355), APOLLO (16612), PARS (VPCV764). January on line with DATAS II SYSTEM I.

AMX, MC, DC, VISA accepted

Panoramic View of Lynn Canal and Portage Cove
ONE OF ALASKA'S FINER MOTELS

Captain's Choice Motel
"24 Luxury Rooms"
P.O. Box 392 • Haines, Alaska 99827 • (907) 766-2461
Your Hosts • Dalton and Gale Hay

Special "Eagle Watcher's" package available October through January. Includes motel accommodations, guided tours through National Eagle Preserve, lunch, round-trip air fare from Juneau-Haines-Juneau, and hundreds of Eagles to photograph!

SUMMERTIME SALMON AND HALIBUT FISHING PACKAGES ALSO AVAILABLE!

Alaska's Tudor Motel/Anchorage
The Best Motel Value in Anchorage!!

One Bedroom Suites for the Price of a Room • Full Kitchen Facilities
Color TV • 20 Channel Cable
Telephones • Hospital Clean
Airport Shuttle Bus
S.E. Corner Lake Otis and Tudor

4423 Lake Otis • Anchorage, AK 99507 •(907) 561-2234

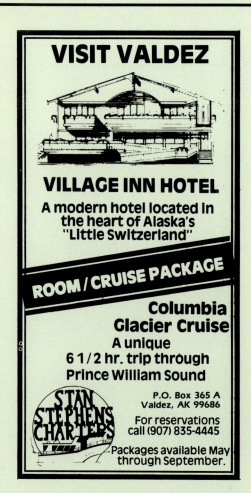

Accommodations (cont'd)

Homer

Driftwood Inn. Homey, historic, uniquely Alaskan 18-room hotel-motel-bed & breakfast. Downtown on scenic, quiet beach; close to everything. Free coffee, video games. Free airport, ferry transportation. Free friendly help arranging fishing, hunting, sightseeing. Specializing in family atmosphere and facilities for the sportsman. Year-round service. Rates $30-$65. Brochure. Write 135-A Bunnell, Homer, AK 99603. (907) 235-8019. "We are what you came to Alaska for!"

Palmer

Russell's Bed & Board. Clean, comfortable guestrooms. Sourdough Pancakes & Pampering. $35, $45 dbl., full-board available. M 37.8 Parks on Gershmel Loop. SRA Box 6229-R, Palmer, AK 99645. (907) 376-7662.

Valdez

Village Inn. (See advertisement this page). PO Box 365, Valdez, AK 99686. (907) 835-4445.

Air Taxi / Flightseeing

Air taxis can be found in most Alaskan communities. They are a quick and easy way to enjoy Alaska's vast roadless wilderness, to get a unique perspective on glaciers and mountains, to visit remote communities, and to fish far from crowded highway streams. In Alaska, where approximately one out of every 40 persons is a registered pilot, there are many skilled (also known as "righteous") aviators. Feel free to ask about an operator's pilot's license, insurance, and safety record.

Arctic and Western

Ambler Air Service. Ambler, AK 99786. (907) 445-2121.

Audi Air. Box 40, Barter Island, AK 99747. (907) 640-6511.

Baker Aviation, Inc. Box 116, Kotzebue, AK 99752. (907) 442-3108.

Bering Air, Inc. Box 1650, Nome AK 99762 (907) 443-5464.

Brooks Range Aviation, Inc. Bettles, AK 99726. (907) 692-5444.

Cape Smythe Air Service. Box 549, Barrow, AK 99723. (907) 852-8333.

Foster Aviation. Box 1028, Nome, AK 99762. (907) 443-5292.

Ryan Air. Daily scheduled passenger flights and freight service to 70 western Alaska communities. 4750 W. International Airport Rd., Anchorage, AK 99518. (907) 562-2227.

Shellabarger Flying Service. Box 11, Kotzebue, AK 99752. (907) 442-3187 or 442-3281.

Sourdough Air Service. Air taxi with over 10 years experience flying in the Brooks Range. Floats, wheels, skis. Trip planning assistance, canoe, kayak, raft, equipment, remote cabin rentals. Year-round service. Air taxi license pending. Brochure. VS, AE, MC accepted. Box 90AB Bettles, AK 99726. (907) 692-5252.

Walker Air Service. Box 57, Kotzebue, AK 99752. (907) 442-3592.

Southcentral and Interior

Alaska Wilderness Travel. (See adventures pgs. 11, 12, 14, 26, 41, 72, 85, & 97) 121 W. Fireweed, Anchorage, AK 99503. (907) 277-7671, 1-800-544-2236.

Alpine Aviation. (See adventure, pg. 25) PO Box 1909, Valdez, AK 99686. (907) 835-4304.

Doug Geeting Aviation. (See adventure pg. 38) PO Box 42A, Talkeetna, AK 99676. (907) 733-2366.

Harbor Air, Inc. (See adventure, pg. 21) PO Box 269, Seward Airport, Seward, AK 99664. (907) 224-3133.

K2 Aviation. (See adventure pg. 37) Expedition support, McKinley flightseeing, charters statewide, wheels, skis, and floats. Brochure. PO Box 290A, Talkeetna, AK 99676. USA Phone (907) 733-2291.

Knik Air, Inc. (See advertisement this page). Box 872145, Wasilla, AK 99687. (907) 376-4888.

Sourdough Air Service. Air taxi with over 10 years experience flying in the Brooks Range. Floats, wheels, skis. Trip planning assistance, canoe, kayak, raft, equipment, remote cabin rentals. Year-round service. Air taxi license pending. Brochure. VS, AE, MC accepted. Box 90AB Bettles, AK 99726. (907) 692-5252.

Talkeetna Air Taxi. (See adventure, pg. 37, see advertisement on next page) PO Box 73, Talkeetna, AK 99676. (907) 733-2218.

Auto/RV Rentals

Like to travel independently? Fly to Alaska and drive the state yourself. Major highways are carefully maintained year round. In the larger cities, you can rent a full range of transportation: compacts, full size sedans, limos, vans, campers and motor homes.

Payment by national credit card is well accepted. If you want to pay by check, phone ahead to get an okay. Reserve early, especially for summer.

Ask about options such as ski racks, linens or housekeeping packages for motor homes, picnic grills, fishing gear and licenses. These can save you a lot of time. RV facilities are usually simple; don't expect luxury campgrounds.

Fuel prices are comparable to similar urban or rural areas in the continental U.S.

Alaska Wilderness Travel. 121 W. Fireweed, Anchorage, AK 99503. (907) 277-7671, 1-800-544-2236.

Anchorage U-Haul Center. Rentals in Alaska, full vacation packages: motorhomes, campers, boats, rafts, camping gear. Call or write for rates and reservations: 4751 Old Seward Highway, Anchorage, AK 99503. (907) 561-2266.

Rent A Wreck. (See advertisement this page). 1313 Laona Circle, Anchorage, AK 99502. (907) 561-2218.

Need a car? "Why not rent one of ours?" "Rent a used car and save."

Outside Alaska
TOLL FREE (800) 544-2288
Inside Alaska
(800) 478-2288

Car in the shop? We'll keep you on the go for less money. "Rent a used truck and save."

— ANCHORAGE INTERNATIONAL —
561-2218

— MERRILL FIELD —
279-9611

— ANCHORAGE DOWNTOWN —
276-8459

— BY THE DAY — WEEK — MONTH

MILITARY DISCOUNTS
NEW CARS AVAILABLE
★ **CASH DEPOSITS WELCOME**
FAIRBANKS DOWNTOWN 456-8459

"Skiers and Flightseers Beneath McKinley"

LOWELL THOMAS, JR.
OWNER/CHIEF PILOT

Ski/Wheel, Float & Turbocharged Aircraft Serving:

- flightseers, skiers & photographers
- wilderness campers, fishermen & hunters
- resource managers & the general public
- mountain climbers thruout the Alaska Range

TALKEETNA AIR TAXI, INC.

MOUNTAIN FLYING and GLACIER LANDINGS A SPECIALTY

Flights From Anchorage & Talkeetna

For Reservations & Information Contact:

TALKEETNA AIR TAXI, INC.
BOX 73-T
TALKEETNA, AK 99676
TELE: (907) 733-2218

"Mt. McKinley, Denali National Park"

Auto/RV Rentals (cont'd)

Sourdough Camper Rentals. To get the feel and flavor of this mighty land, flying is not enough! In the comfort of our motorhomes, experiencing Alaska firsthand can be the thrill of a lifetime! Our self-contained units range from truck campers to 30-foot Class A motorhomes. Housekeeping packages and convenience items available. Free airport transportation also available. Write for our free brochure: Sourdough Camper Rentals, Box 92440, Anchorage, AK 99509. (907) 563-3268.

Thrifty Car Rental. Sub-compact to full-size cars available; mini vans, 7-passenger and 12-passenger vans available. Free airport, railroad, dock and downtown pick-up service. Daily and weekly rates that include mileage. Brochure available. VS, AE, MC, DC, CB, DIS. accepted. Write 3730-AAB Spenard Rd., Anchorage, AK. 99517. (907) 276-2855 or 800-FOR-CARS for reservations and information.

Birding

Bring your binoculars! There are over 400 bird species in Alaska, about two-thirds of which are migratory. Bald eagles, endangered elsewhere in the U.S., are common in Alaska wherever there are salmon.

By road you can reach wetlands with thousands of migratory waterfowl. The Potter Point State Game Refuge in Anchorage or the Creamer's Field Waterfowl Refuge in Fairbanks are good places to see a variety of species including arctic terns, Canada geese, and dabbling and diving ducks. The Chilkat Bald Eagle Preserve near Haines is frequented by thousands of eagles gathering to feed on salmon.

Alaska Wilderness Travel. 121 W. Fireweed, Anchorage, AK 99503. (907) 277-7671, 1-800-544-2236.

Alaskan Sojourns. (See adventure, pg. 22) PO Box 87-1410, Wasilla, AK 99687. (907) 376-2913.

Saint George Tanaq. (See adventure, pg. 91) 2604 Fairbanks St., Anchorage, AK 99503. (907) 276-3600.

Silver Salmon Creek Lodge. (See adventure, pg. 17) PO Box 3234, Soldotna, AK 99669. (907) 262-4839.

Wilderness Birding Adventures. (See adventure, pg. 65) PO Box 103747, Anchorage, AK 99510-3747. (907) 694-7442.

Bus Tours

Motorcoach driver/guides will fill you in on history, geology, flora, and fauna while you relax and enjoy the scenery.

In most larger Alaskan communities you have a choice between large, modern motorcoaches and smaller, more personalized tour services. City tours show you the sights of any of Alaska's larger cities in 2 to 3 hours. Or you can arrange to travel beyond the city to enjoy glaciers, parks, wildlife and scenery.

Combined air and motorcoach tours whisk you by jet or turboprop to destinations such as Nome, Kotzebue, Kodiak, Barrow, Katmai, and Glacier Bay. Tour attractions vary with the destination: gold mining and dog mushing in Nome, Native dancing and folk tales in Kotzebue, wildlife and geology in Katmai.

Alaska Wilderness Travel. (See adventure pg. 63) 121 W. Fireweed, Anchorage, AK 99503. (907) 277-7671, 1-800-544-2236.

Kodiak Island Tours. Bus/Charter & Sightseeing. Superior first class escorted motor coach tours of Kodiak Island with guaranteed departure dates. Box 5509, Chiniak, AK 99615. (907) 486-4467.

Mt. McKinley Alaska Glacier Tours. Economical around All-Alaska adventures and car rental driving holidays. Examples: Two-day Denali Park from $139; Two-day Columbia Glacier from $190. Send for flyer. 608 West 4th Avenue, PO Box 102315, Anchorage, AK 99510. Telephone (907) 274-8539.

Camping (See "Hiking/Camping")

Climate & Clothing

Alaska takes in maritime, transition, continental, and arctic climates.

When packing for an Alaskan vacation keep in mind that the weather is unpredictable and may change several times in the course of a day. If you're dressing for the outdoors, wear or bring several layers of clothing to add or shed as the weather dictates. Polypropylene clothing, available at many outdoor stores, is very popular in Alaska. It is light and comfortable and it doesn't lose its ability to keep you warm when wet. Pyle jackets and hats are popular for the same reasons. Cotton, by comparison, is a very poor insulator when it gets wet. Your outer layer should include waterproof and windproof shells and a wool cap if you plan to venture very far from shelter. Long sleeves and scarves or bandanas can offer added protection from insects.

City dress is decidedly casual throughout Alaska. Slacks with shirt or blouse are adequate for most nightlife activity.

Cruises

Alaska Wilderness Travel. (See adventure, pg. 99) 121 W. Fireweed, Anchorage, AK 99503. (907) 277-7671, 1-800-544-2236.

Dogsled

Alaska Treks Unlimited. Dogmushing is our specialty. Personal tours for those seeking a unique Alaskan experience. Active participation at any skill level. We also provide skier and mountaineer group support, ice fishing and other winter pursuits. Nov. 15 - Apr. 15. Brochure. Write: Box 82655-A, Fairbanks, AK 99708. (907) 455-6326.

Alaska Wilderness Travel. (See adventure, pg. 39) 121 W. Fireweed, Anchorage, AK 99503. (907) 277-7671, 1-800-544-2236.

Brooks Range Wilderness Trips. (See adventure, pg. 57) PO Box 48A, Bettles, AK 99726. (907) 692-5312.

Susitna Dog Tours. (See adventure, pg. 13) Box 404-G, Willow, AK 99688. (907) 495-6324, (800) 544-2235.

Fishing

As Alaskans grow more conservation minded the mark of sportfishing savvy is not how many fish one catches, but how skillfully one handles and releases a fish. "Catch and release" fishing is a common practice for certain kinds of fish which reproduce slowly--rainbow trout, for example. By contrast it is widely accepted to take home the legal limit of salmon. To improve your fishing success rate: 1) Wear polaroid sunglasses to cut the water's glare, 2) sharpen (and even de-barb) your hooks, and 3) wet your knots before you tighten them.

Fishing regulations may be obtained at most sporting goods stores or from the Alaska Dept. of Fish and Game, 333 Raspberry Rd., Anchorage, AK 99518. (907) 267-2218. Fishing licenses are required for anyone 16 years and older, and may be obtained at almost any sporting goods store. Non-resident fishing license rates are: 3-day--$10, 14-day--$20, 1-year--$36. Resident licenses are $10, valid for the calendar year issued. For regularly updated Southcentral Alaska fishing reports call (907) 349-4687.

Alaska River & Ski Tours, Inc. (See adventure pgs. 13, 72) Come with Alaska's most respected full service adventure outfitters. We are year round residents and know the backcountry well. Let us take you someplace special. *Alaska's best fishing *Wildwater trips *World class hikes *Wild and scenic rivers *Explore Alaska's coastline by kayak *Dog team supported x/c ski tours. Free brochure call or write: 1831 Kuskokwim St., Suite C, Anchorage, AK 99508. (907) 276-3418, Telex 25-147.

Fishing (cont'd)

Alaska Wilderness Travel. (See adventures, pgs. 11, 12, 14, 17, 18, 59, 98) 121 W. Fireweed, Anchorage, AK 99503. (907) 277-7671, 1-800-544-2236.

Alaska Wilderness Co-op. (See adventures, pgs. 69, 71, 85) 4341 MacAlister Dr., Anchorage, AK 99515. (907) 243-3068.

Brightwater Alaska. (See adventures, pgs. 30, 85) Guided and outfitted trophy fishing float trips on the finest waters in Bristol Bay since 1975. Salmon, rainbow, char, dolly varden, grayling, pike. Small groups with emphasis on fishing and enjoyment. Brochure upon request. Commissionable. PO Box 110796-A, Anchorage, AK 99511. (907) 243-1922.

Gone Fishing. (See adventure pg. 71) William R. Lyle, PO Box 589, Wasilla, AK 99687. (907) 376-6514.

Johnson Brothers Guides & Outfitters. (See adventure, pg. 18) 44526 Sterling Hwy., Soldotna, AK 99669. (907) 262-5357.

Knik Air, Inc. (See advertisement, page 108). Air transportation to all points in Alaska. Year round operation equipped with wheels, skis and floats. Convenient pickup in Anchorage. Experience the true Alaska with the experts in flying the Alaska bush. Box 872145, Wasilla, AK 99687. (907) 376-4888.

Painter Creek Lodge. (See adventure, pg. 87) Box 1350, Palmer, AK 99645. (907) 745-3772.

Stephan Lake Lodge. (See advertisement, this page). PO Box 695, Eagle River, AK 99577. (907) 688-2163.

Fishing Derbies

Valdez Fishing Derbies. (See adventure, pg. 25) Valdez Chamber of Commerce, PO Box 512, Valdez, AK 99686. (907) 835-2330.

Hiking/Camping/Backpacking

Most visitors to Alaska stick to the roads, which means that hiking or backpacking can be a great way to see the state. Always be prepared for the worst possible weather--windproof and waterproof shells are a necessity. Traveling with a friend also makes good sense.

Most large tracts of public lands are open to wilderness camping, though many of these lands are inhospitable due to swamps, thick undergrowth or insects in certain seasons. You will need to obtain permits in Denali National Park and some other parks. Open fires are often prohibited because the tundra grows back very slowly. In Denali Park, a free shuttle bus system will drop you off and pick you up at half-hour intervals anywhere along the road. Some areas are intermittently closed to camping due to increased bear activity. For more information see "Parks and Public Lands."

A guided backpacking or camping trip can be a great buy when you consider the logistical planning and gear preparation required for an Alaskan wilderness trip. It can also be a great school for learning Alaskan wilderness skills. Don't be shy about questioning an outfitter as regards his/her experience or asking for references from past clients.

Alaska-Denali Guiding, Inc. Join us for a wilderness trek in remote areas of Alaska. We specialize in custom trips. For brochure write: Brian and Diane Okonek, Box 326, Talkeetna, AK 99676. (907) 733-2649.

Alaska Wilderness Travel. (See adventures, pgs. 35, 61) 121 W. Fireweed, Anchorage, AK 99503. (907) 277-7671, 1-800-544-2236.

Alaska Wilderness Co-op. (See adventures, pgs. 53, 57, 59, 65) 4341 MacAlister Dr., Anchorage, AK 99515. (907) 243-3068.

CampAlaska. (See adventure, pg. 14) PO Box 872247, Wasilla, AK 99687. (907) 376-9438.

Distant Shores. Spectacular Lake Clark National Park. Guided boating, hiking, photography, wildlife, exploring. Comfortable tent camps. Private parties, secluded environment. Affordable wilderness experience. 421-AB W. 88th, Anchorage, AK 99515. (907) 349-4239.

Hugh Glass Backpacking Company. (See adventures, pgs. 30, 85) Small group adventures statewide since 1975. Emphasis on wildlife, scenery, interpretation and enjoyment. Brooks Range, Wrangells, Lake Clark, and more. (See ad in "Outfitters" section.) Commissionable. PO Box 110796-A, Anchorage, AK 99511. (907) 243-1922.

Greatland Travel Guides. Denali Southside. Guided tours featuring Denali National and State parks. Year-round adventures; fishing, rafting, backpacking, dog-sledding, skiing. Contact: Box 1480, Talkeetna, AK 99676. (907) 733-2821.

Wilderness Alaska. (See adventure, pg. 65) 6710 Potter Heights, Anchorage, AK 99516. (907) 345-3366.

Wilderness: Alaska/Mexico. Brooks Range Adventures. Backpack, Klepper kayak and cross-country ski trips in the Gates of the Arctic, Arctic National Wildlife Refuge & Noatak National Preserve. 18 years experience. 1231-AAB Sundance Loop, Fairbanks, AK 99709. (907) 452-1821.

Horse Rides

Alaska Wilderness Travel. (See adventure, pg. 31) 121 W. Fireweed, Anchorage, AK 99503. (907) 277-7671, 1-800-544-2236.

Southfork Outfit. Guided and outfitted horseback tours daily or overnight for all ages and experience. Established camps in the Talkeetna and Chugach mountains. Located on Sheep Mountain Game Reserve, Mile 111.5 Glenn Hwy. Mark Meekin, SRC Box 8488A, Palmer, AK 99645. (907) 745-5143.

Hunting

Hunting regulations may be obtained at most sporting goods stores or from the Alaska Dept. of Fish and Game, 333 Raspberry Rd., Anchorage, AK 99518. (907) 344-0541. For a regularly updated Southcentral hunting information recording call (907) 349-4687.

Alaska Wilderness Travel. (See adventure, pg. 72) 121 W. Fireweed, Anchorage, AK 99503. (907) 277-7671, 1-800-544-2236.

Big Boys Toys. We have everything you need to make your hunting trip an enjoyable event, from ATV's to snowmachines - complete outfitters! Reserve your equipment early! 6511 Brayton, Anchorage, AK 99507. (907) 349-1425.

STEPHAN LAKE LODGE

A fly-in wilderness lodge, located in the interior of Alaska, **Stephan Lake Lodge** specializes in your enjoyment . . . from the home cooked meals on a wood-burning stove at the lodge to the seven outlying log cabins for

HUNTING, FISHING, HIKING, PHOTO TRIPS, RAFTING and WINTER ACTIVITIES.

We hunt **KODIAK** also!

JIM BAILEY, Registered Guide
P.O. Box 695 • Eagle River, Alaska 99577
(907) 688-2163

Hunting (con't)

Knik Air, Inc. (See advertisement, page 108). Air transportation to all points in Alaska. Year round operation equipped with wheels, skis and floats. Convenient pickup in Anchorage. Experience the true Alaska with the experts in flying the Alaska bush. Box 872145, Wasilla, AK 99687. (907) 376-4888.

Exclusive Alaska Hunts. (See advertisement this page). SRC Box 8860, Palmer, AK 99645.

Stephan Lake Lodge. (See advertisement this page.) PO Box 695, Eagle River, AK 99577. (907) 688-2163.

STEPHAN LAKE LODGE

A fly-in wilderness lodge, located in the interior of Alaska, **Stephan Lake Lodge** specializes in your enjoyment . . . from the home cooked meals on a wood-burning stove at the lodge to the seven outlying log cabins for
HUNTING, FISHING, HIKING, PHOTO TRIPS, RAFTING and WINTER ACTIVITIES.
We hunt **KODIAK** also!
JIM BAILEY, Registered Guide
P.O. Box 695 • Eagle River, Alaska 99577
(907) 688-2163

Exclusive Alaskan Hunts

Andy Runyan
Master Guide

Fair-chase Hunts

Brown Bear
Caribou   Blacktail

Alaska Peninsula and Kodiak

Please Write:
Star Rte. C • Box 8860
Palmer, Alaska 99645

Lodges / Rustic Cabins

Afognak Cabins. (See adventure, pg. 81) Unguided, remote accommodations with air and ocean access. Hunting, fishing, photography and sightseeing. Roomy, yet cozy, cabins have six bunks, and oil heating and cooking facilities. June through December. 413 Rezanof Drive East, Kodiak, AK 99615. (907) 486-6014.

Alaska Wilderness Travel. (See adventures, pgs. 35, 53) 121 W. Fireweed, Anchorage, AK 99503. (907) 277-7671, 1-800-544-2236.

Bristol Bay Lodge. (See adventure, pg. 72; see advertisement this page). PO Box 190349, Anchorage, AK 99519. (907) 248-1714.

Glacier Bay Country Inn. Secluded retreat offers the chance to really experience Alaskan country living--away from the crowds and in a wilderness setting. Home-baked breads, garden-fresh produce, local seafoods. Private baths. Glacier Bay boat/plane tours, fishing charters. Special package rates available. Box 5-AA, Gustavus, AK 99826. (907) 697-2288.

Golden Horn Lodge. (See adventure, pg. 71) PO Box 6748, Anchorage, AK 99502. (907) 243-1455.

Gracious House Lodge and Flying Service. (See adventure pg. 39) 859 Elaine Dr., Anchorage, AK 99504. (907) 333-3148.

Hatcher Pass Lodge. (See adventure, pg. 14) Box 2655-F, Palmer, AK 99645. (907) 745-5897.

Mystic Lake Lodge. (See adventure, pg. 37) George Palmer, Box 887, Palmer, AK 99645. (907) 745-3168.

Riversong Lodge. (See adventure, pg. 12) Skwentna, AK 99667. (907) 733-2931.

Sheep Mountain Lodge. (See advertisement this page). SRC Box 8490, Palmer, AK 99645. (907) 745-5121.

Silvertip Lodges. PO Box 190389, Anchorage, AK 99519-0389. (907) 248-0149.

Saint Elias Alpine Guides. (See adventure, pg. 29) Box 111241, Anchorage, AK 99511. (907) 277-6867.

Thayer Lake Lodge. (See adventure, pg. 98) PO Box 5416, Ketchikan, AK 99901. (907) 225-3343, 225-6371, 789-0944, or 789-5646.

Mountaineering

Alaska-Denali Guiding, Inc. Mt. McKinley and Alaska Range expeditions, mountaineering seminars and custom climbs. For brochure, write: Brian and Diane Okonek, Box 326, Talkeetna, AK 99676. (907) 733-2649.

Alaska Wilderness Travel. (See adventure, pg. 53) 121 W. Fireweed, Anchorage, AK 99503. (907) 277-7671, 1-800-544-2236.

Genet Expeditions. (See adventure, pg. 38) Climb Mt. McKinley, North America's highest peak. Ski the spectacular Ruth Glacier, stay in the Don Sheldon Mountain Hut and enjoy gourmet cooking. Climb and ski in the Wrangell Mountains. Special youth adventures. Call or write: Genet Expeditions, Talkeetna, AK 99676. (907) 376-5120.

Mountain Trip. (See adventure, pg. 38) Gary Bocarde, Box 91161, Anchorage, AK 99509. (907) 345-6499.

St. Elias Alpine Guides. (See adventure, pg. 29) Box 111241, Anchorage, AK 99511. (907) 277-6867.

Sheep Mountain Lodge
Homecooked Meals
Bar • Liquor Store • Cabins
Camping • Sauna • Hot Tub
Hiking Trails · X-Country Skiing
Open Year-round
SRC Box 8490, Palmer, AK. 99645
Mile 113.5 Glenn Hwy
(907) 745-5121

Bristol Bay Lodge
Angling Accommodations

Experience the best of Alaskan sportfishing with one of Alaska's oldest, most experienced fly-out wilderness lodges. World-wide references.

Ron McMillan • P.O. Box 190349 • Anchorage, AK 99519
(907) 248-1714 Oct. through May
(907) 842-2500 June through Sept.

Museums / Galleries

Baranov Museum. In the Erskine House, a National Historic Landmark in downtown Kodiak. The Erskine House served as a warehouse for furs and as office of the manager of the Russian American Company. 101 Marine Way, Kodiak, AK 99615. (907) 486-5920.

Last Frontier Gallery. (See advertisement this page). PO Box 587, Valdez, AK 99686. (907) 835-4959.

Museum of Alaska Transportation & Industry. (See adventure, pg. 13) PO Box 909, Palmer, AK 99645. (907) 745-4493.

Natural and Cultural History Museum of Alaska. (See advertisement this page). University of Alaska, Fairbanks, 907 Yukon Drive, Fairbanks, AK 99775-1200. (907) 474-7505.

Nature Tours

Alaska Cross Country Guiding and Rafting. (See adventure, pg. 103) Box 124, Haines, AK 99827.

Alaska Discovery. (See adventure, pg. 101) Completely outfitted 4-14 day adventures by touring kayak, raft, backpack, & canoe into Glacier Bay, Admiralty Island Wilderness, Tatshenshini river & other outstanding wildlands. Send for listing of scheduled trips & custom itineraries. PO Box 021892-A, Juneau, AK 99801. (907) 586-1911.

Alaska Sea Kayaking. (See adventure, pg. 27) Box 1386, Palmer, AK 99645. (907) 745-3487.

Alaska Treks N Voyages. Steve Hackett, PO Box 600, Moose Pass, AK 99631. (907) 288-3610 or 224-3960.

Alaska Wilderness Travel. (See adventures, pgs. 26, 59, 101) 121 W. Fireweed, Anchorage, AK 99503. (907) 277-7671, 1-800-544-2236.

Alaska Wilderness Co-op. (See adventures, pgs. 43, 61, 71) 4341 MacAlister Dr., Anchorage, AK 99515. (907) 243-3068.

Alaskan Sojourns. (See adventure, pg. 22) PO Box 87-1410, Wasilla, AK 99687. (907) 376-2913.

Greatland Travel Guides. Denali Southside. Guided tours featuring Denali National and State parks. Year-round adventures; fishing, rafting, backpacking, dog-sledding, skiing. Contact: Box 1480, Talkeetna, AK 99676. (907) 733-2821.

The Natural and Cultural History Museum of Alaska

Rated as one of the top 10 attractions in the state. Alaska's largest gold collection. *Blue Babe*. A restored 36,000 year old steppe bison. Museum. Store. Gifts. T-shirts. Mail order catalog available.

university of alaska Museum
fairbanks (907) 474-7505

907 yukon drive, fairbanks, alaska 99775-1200

Helen Greets You

Cama'i Alaska "Yupik-Eskimo"
Come by for a Visit
Gifts—Local Crafts—Ivory
Alaska Paintings & Prints

Last Frontier Gallery
P.O. Box 587 Valdez, Alaska 99686
907-835-4959

Kenai Fjords Tours, Inc. (See adventure, pg. 21) Box 1889AA, Seward, AK 99664. (907) 224-8068 or 224-3668.

Wilderness Air Tours of Alaska. (See adventure, pg. 11) Call us when you get to Anchorage and we'll schedule you for the next good tour day (weatherwise). Ask about our "no-fish, no-pay" guided fishing trips. No reservations or deposits necessary. Cash or travelers checks only, payable before tour begins. Our airplanes are based at Birchwood Airport, 21 miles north of Anchorage, just off the Glenn Hwy. Brochure. PO Box 770032, Eagle River, AK 99577. (907) 688-2478.

Ocean Charters

Alaska Sea Adventures. (See adventure, pg. 97) 318 Coleman Dr., Juneau, AK 99801. (907) 586-1947, 1-800-252-7527.

Alaska Wilderness Travel. (See adventure, pg. 98) 121 W. Fireweed, Anchorage, AK 99503. (907) 277-7671, 1-800-544-2236.

Camai Yacht Charters. (See advertisement, pg. 22) 12800 Saunders Rd., Anchorage AK 99516. (907) 333-1916 or (907) 345-2100.

Choice Marine Charters. (See adventure, pg. 26) Serving Prince William Sound. Fishing, sightseeing, hunting, kayak drop-off, overnight and extended excursions, Whittier departures. April-December. PO Box 200592, Anchorage, AK 99520-0592. (907) 243-0069.

Good Time Charters. Saltwater trolling for the largest King salmon in the world. Superb halibut fishing, clamdigging, cookouts, bed & breakfast, Homer tours. See glaciers, volcano, world's second largest natural spit of land. Homer is the "Shangri-la of Alaska". Half-day, all-day, combo charters, outrigger/downrigger equipped. Personal attention from owner/operator, lifetime Homer resident, Coast Guard licensed skipper--Jeff Cundiff, HCR 67865 Virginia Avenue, Homer, AK 99603. (907) 235-7346.

Homer Ocean Charters, Inc. (See adventure, pg. 17) Located on Homer Spit, Cannery Row Boardwalk. Call or write for free brochure. Make reservations early. Box 2543, Homer, AK 99603. (907) 235-6212.

Mariah Charters. (See adventure pg. 22, see advertisement this page). Full color brochure and price list available upon request. 3812 Katmai Circle, Anchorage, AK 99503. (907) 243-1238.

Pier 34 Charters. Fishing, sightseeing, birdwatching, whalewatching. Wilderness drop-offs. Overnighters. Boats from 25-70+ feet, available year round. We have sailboats, too. For the "adventure of a lifetime", write: Box 2416, Seward, AK 99664. (907) 224-3474.

Sitka's Secrets. Personable boat charters. Maximum accommodations, four adults. Unforgettable adventures with marine wildlife. Whales, otters, seabirds, salmon, halibut, crabs. $70/day/adult. Brochure. Write: Box 950-A, Sitka, AK 99835.

Stan Stevens Charters. (See adventure, pg. 25) PO Box 1297, Valdez, AK 99686. (907) 835-4731.

Mariah Charters
WE OPERATE IN SOME OF THE MOST BEAUTIFUL MARINE ENVIRONMENT FOUND IN ALASKA: KENAI FJORDS NTL. PARK, NORTH GULF COAST, AND PRINCE WILLIAM SOUND.
FISHING • TOURING • DROP-OFF/PICKUP
COAST GUARD INSPECTED AND LICENSED

For Prices & Reservations — John Sheedy, Skipper/Owner
Mariah Charters
3812 Katmai Circle
Anchorage, Alaska 99503
(907) 243-1238

Ocean Kayaking

Ageya Kayak Tours. (See adventure, pg. 21) 2517 Foraker Dr., Anchorage, AK 99517. (907) 248-7140.

Alaska Sea Kayaking. (See adventure, pg. 27) Box 1386, Palmer, AK 99645. (907) 745-3487.

Alaska Discovery. (See adventure, pg. 101) Completely outfitted adventures by touring kayak into Glacier Bay. Send for listing of scheduled trips & custom itineraries. PO Box 021892-A, Juneau, AK 99801. (907)586-1911.

Alaska Treks n Voyages. (See advertisement this page). Sea kayak rentals, instruction tours, and charter boat drop-off/pick-ups in Resurrection Bay, S. Western Prince William Sound, and to all parts of the Kenai Fjords National Park highlight our Seward-based operations. Scheduled day hikes, longer backpacking treks with packdogs, glacier trips and summer skiing in adjacent Kenai Mountains. Small Boat Harbor, PO Box 625, Seward, AK. 99664. (907) 224-3960 or 288-3610.

Alaska Wilderness Travel. 121 W. Fireweed, Anchorage, AK 99503. (907) 277-7671, 1-800-544-2236.

Hugh Glass Backpacking Company. (See adventures, pgs. 30 & 85) Experience the beauty and abundance of Alaska's richest ecosystem. Small group adventures into Kenai Fjords National Park and Prince William Sound. No experience necessary. (See ad in "Outfitters" section.) Commissionable. PO Box 110796-A, Anchorage, AK 99511. (907) 243-1922.

Siwash Safaris. (See adventure, pg. 18) 2312 Loussac, Anchorage, AK 99517. (907) 248-0222.

Wilderness Alaska. (See adventure, pg. 65) 6710 Potter Heights, Anchorage, AK 99516. (907) 345-3366.

KAYAK THE FJORDS!

Sea Kayaking in
Kenai Fjords Nat'l. Park

Packdog Treks —
Statewide Expeditions

Alaska TREKS n VOYAGES
P.O. Box 625-B
Seward, ALASKA 99664
(907) 224-3960

Outdoor Education

Alaska Wilderness Travel. (See adventure, pg. 103) 121 W. Fireweed, Anchorage, AK 99503. (907) 277-7671, 1-800-544-2236.

Mountain Trip. (See adventure, pg. 38) Gary Bocarde, Box 91161, Anchorage, AK 99509. (907) 345-6499.

Outdoor Equipment Rental

Big Boys Toys. (See advertisement this page). 6511 Brayton Dr., Anchorage, AK 99507. (907) 349-1425.

Alaska Treks N Voyages. Steve Hackett, PO Box 600, Moose Pass, AK 99631. (907) 288-3610 or 224-3960.

Outfitters

Alaska Treks n Voyages. Scheduled and custom one-day to two-week adventure trips throughout Alaska's parklands. Completely outfitted mountain treks and river voyages to most parts of the state: Brooks Range and North Slope above the Arctic Circle; dogsled and packdog tours in the Alaska Range near Mt. McKinley; backpacking and river trips in Aleutian Range and Lake Clark region. All inclusive from Fairbanks, Anchorage or Seward. AWGA certified outfitter. Steve Hackett, Director. PO Box 600, Moose Pass, AK 99631. (907) 288-3610.

Alaska Wilderness Travel. 121 W. Fireweed, Anchorage, AK 99503. (907) 277-7671, 1-800-544-2236.

Big Boys Toys. Explore the majesty of Alaska from an ATV! Fish - hunt - take a canoe or raft trip down an exciting river! Complete outfitters for all outdoor recreation needs. 6511 Brayton, Anchorage, AK 99507. (907) 349-1425.

Brooks Range Expeditions. (See advertisement this page). General Delivery, Bettles Field, AK 99726. (907) 692-5333.

Hugh Glass Backpacking Company. (See adventures, pgs. 30 & 85) Guided and outfitted wilderness adventures since 1975. Treks, river trips, ocean kayaking, trophy fishing. Top quality small group trips into Alaska's finest wilderness areas. Emphasis on scenery, wildlife, exploration, interpretation, and enjoyment. Custom trips available. Brochure on request. Commissionable. PO Box 110796-A, Anchorage, AK 99511. (907) 243-1922.

BIG BOYS TOYS

Recreational **RENTALS** And Outfitting

- ATV's
- Boats & Motors
- Dry Suits
- Golf Equip.
- Jet - Skis
- Mountain Bikes
- Rafts / Canoes
- Water Skis

6511 Brayton Dr.
Anchorage, AK 99507

349-1425

Advance Equipment Reservations Recommended to insure availablity.

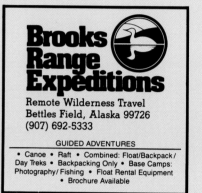

Brooks Range Expeditions

Remote Wilderness Travel
Bettles Field, Alaska 99726
(907) 692-5333

GUIDED ADVENTURES
- Canoe • Raft • Combined: Float/Backpack/
Day Treks • Backpacking Only • Base Camps:
Photography/ Fishing • Float Rental Equipment
• Brochure Available

Sourdough Outfitters. Specializing in Brooks Range wilderness trips since 1974. Backpack Arrigetch Peaks and Gates of the Arctic. Canoe, raft or kayak Noatak, Kobuk, Koyukuk, Alatna and other rivers. Dog sled and XC ski February - April. Wildlife base camps, canoe and equipment rental, wilderness cabins. Year-round service. Guided/unguided. Brochure. VS, MC, AE accepted. Write: Box 90AB, Bettles, AK 99726. (907) 692-5252.

Parks / Public Lands

Public Interest Lands (parks, wildlife refuges, etc.) comprise over forty percent of Alaska's total land mass. You can get visitor information from agencies listed below. They will refer you if another office has the information you need. It's best to write ahead for information. When telephoning, remember Alaska Time, for most of the state, is: one hour later than Hawaiian; one hour earlier than Pacific; two hours earlier than Mountain; three hours earlier than Central; four hours earlier than Eastern.

State of Alaska:

State Parks: Division of Parks, Alaska Dept. of Natural Resources, Box 7007, Anchorage, AK 99510. (907) 561-2020, 762-4565.

Parks / Public Lands (con't)

U. S. Government agencies:

National parks, monuments and preserves: National Park Service, U.S. Department of the Interior, 2525 Gambell Street, Room 101, Anchorage, AK 99503. (907) 271-2643.

National forests: U.S. Forest Service, Department of Agriculture, 201 East 9th Avenue, Suite 206, Anchorage, AK 99501. (907) 271-2599.

BLM Lands: Bureau of Land Management, U.S. Department of the Interior, 701 C Street, PO Box 13, Anchorage, AK 99513. (907) 271-5960.

Wildlife refuges: U.S. Fish and Wildlife Service, Department of the Interior, 1011 E. Tudor Road, Anchorage, AK 99503. (907) 786-3487.

Publications

Alaska Paddling Guide. Comprehensive guidebook and sketch maps to over 100 streams and lakes throughout Alaska. 113 pages. $8.95 postpaid. Alaska Float Trips, Box 140264, Anchorage, AK 99514. (907) 333-4442.

Rafting

With more than 3,000 rivers (including 25 National Wild and Scenic Rivers), Alaska offers lots of options for enjoying remote wilderness, wildlife, and fishing.

Alaska Float Trips. Experience Alaska's wildlife, fishing, natural history and scenic grandeur by raft or canoe. 1/2 - 10 day scheduled or customized trips. Family packages. Raft rentals. Brochure. Box 140264, Anchorage, AK 99514. (907) 333-4442.

Alaska River & Ski Tours, Inc. (See adventures, pgs. 13 & 72) Fishing, wildwater trips, wild and scenic rivers Free brochure. 1831 Kuskokwim St., Suite C, Anchorage, AK 99508. (907) 276-3418, Telex 25-147.

Alaska Whitewater. (See adventure, pg. 31) PO Box 142294, Anchorage, AK 99514. (907) 338-0471.

Alaska Wilderness Co-op. (See adventures, pgs. 29, 43, 57, 69, 71, 85, 101) Specialty trips statewide. Indicate areas of interest upon inquiry. 4341 MacAlister Dr., Anchorage, AK 99515. (907) 243-3068.

BIG BOYS TOYS

Recreational **RENTALS** And Outfitting
- ATV's
- Boats & Motors
- Dry Suits
- Golf Equip.
- Jet - Skis
- Mountain Bikes
- Rafts / Canoes
- Water Skis

6511 Brayton Dr.
Anchorage, AK 99507

349-1425

Advance Equipment Reservations Recommended to insure availablity.

Alaska Wilderness Travel. (See adventures, pgs. 12, 14, 31) 121 W. Fireweed, Anchorage, AK 99503. (907) 277-7671, 1-800-544-2236.

Arctic Brotherhood Entertainment Committee. ABEC's Adventures in the Arctic. Paddle raft, kayak and backpack the Brooks Range. Explore Lake Clark National Park. Float the Noatak and Kongakut rivers. Experience Alaska's finest! ABEC, 1304-AAB Westwick Drive, Fairbanks, AK 99712. (907) 457-8907.

Big Boys Toys. (See advertisement this page.) 6511 Brayton Dr., Anchorage, AK 99507. (907) 349-1425.

Hugh Glass Backpacking Company. (See adventures, pgs. 30, 85) Small group raft, canoe and ocean kayaking adventures since 1975. Emphasis on scenery, wildlife, interpretation and enjoyment. (See ad in "Outfitters" section.) Commissionable. PO Box 110796-A, Anchorage, AK 99511. (907) 243-1922.

Keystone Adventures. Raft and kayak trips. Specializing in whitewater, fishing, hunting, hiking, and helicopter-raft trips. One day to twelve day adventures available. PO Box 1486, Valdez, AK 99686. (907) 835-2606.

Nova Riverrunners. (See adventure, pg. 35) SRC Box 8337/Chickaloon, Palmer, AK 99645. (907) 745-5753.

Sailing

Alaska Wilderness Sailing Safaris. (See adventure, pg. 27) PO Box 1313, Valdez, AK 99686. (907) 835-5175.

Camai Yacht Charters. (See adventure, pg. 22; see advertisement this page) 12800 Saunders Rd., Anchorage AK 99516. (907) 333-1916 or (907) 345-2100.

CAMAI YACHT CHARTERS

Sightseeing & Sailing
Luxurious 55 Ft.
Custom Built Ketch

Located in Seward, Alaska

- DAILY SIGHTSEEING & SAILING TOURS
- OVERNIGHT CHARTERS
- EXTENDED CRUISES

(907) 333-1916
or
(907) 345-2100

12800 Saunders Road
Anchorage, Alaska 99516

Shopping/Gifts

Puffin Gift Shop. Alaskan gifts, gold nugget and ivory jewelry. Open year round. Mail orders welcome. Fresh flowers for all your special occasions. Box 2084, Valdez, AK 99686. (907) 835-2288.

Harbor Landing General Store. (See advertisement this page). PO Box 872, Valdez, AK 99686. (907) 835-5228.

HARBOR LANDING GENERAL STORE

UNIQUE VALDEZ GIFTS
"A Paradise for Browsers and Buyers"

ALASKAN JEWELRY AND SOUVENIRS
Many custom made gifts, T-shirts and jackets not found elsewhere.
BEST SELECTION
BEST PRICES

Complimentary Coffee & Spiced Tea
Always Simmering

Located in Harbor Court Near the Gazebo
(One minute walk across Highway from Village Inn.)

(907) 835-5228

One coupon per family, please.
Present this ad for 10% off
any one item of your choice.

Shopping/Gifts (con't)

Wayne's Meat Market. (See advertisement this page). 405 W. Benson Blvd., Anchorage, AK 99503. (907) 561-5135.

Skiing/ Ski Touring

Alaska-Denali Guiding, Inc. See adventure, pg. 39). For brochure write: Brian and Diane Okonek, Box 326, Talkeetna, AK 99676. (907) 733-2649.

Travel Information/Agencies

The Alaska Division of Tourism's 1987 Vacation Planner is a free 112-page book of photos and information covering every region in the state. Listings include transportation, accommodations, activities and attractions, and visitor information sources. Write PO Box E-001, Juneau, AK 99811. (907) 465-2010.

Communities over 2,000 people usually have a Convention and Visitors Bureau or Chamber of Commerce which provides visitor information about their community. These visitor information centers have helpful staff and volunteers who can be of great assistance in helping you plan your trip.

Many public agencies have information centers in and near national and state parks, forests, wildlife refuges and preserves. For more information see "Parks and Public Lands."

Alaska Wilderness Travel. 121 W. Fireweed, Anchorage, AK 99503. (907) 277-7671, 1-800-544-2236.

Anchorage Convention and Visitors Bureau. 201 East Third Avenue, Anchorage, AK 99501. (907) 276-4118. Telex 0353743.

Fairbanks Convention and Visitors Bureau. 550 First Avenue, Fairbanks, AK 99701. (907) 456-5774.

Kodiak Island Convention and Visitors Bureau. 100 Marine Way, Suite 100, Kodiak, AK 99615. (907) 486-4782.

Matanuska-Susitna Convention & Visitors Bureau. (See advertisement this page). Our resort area covers 23,000 square miles! Come up this winter and try ice fishing, dog sled racing, snowmachining, X-country skiing...or plan to enjoy our summer sports, including the best salmon fishing in the state, boating, water skiing, flightseeing, mountain climbing and much more. Rustic or deluxe accomodations. Write for information: Matanuska-Susitna Convention and Visitors Bureau, PO Box 875747-B, Wasilla, AK 99687.

ALASKA TASTES GREAT!

SMOKED SALMON
WILD GAME SAUSAGE
ALASKAN SEAFOOD

HALIBUT – KING CRAB – SHRIMP – SALMON

Enjoy a real taste of Alaska's Bounty. We do custom processing - smoking - packing of your catch, or pick-up some of ours.

Wayne's MEAT MARKET
405 W. Benson • Anchorage, AK • 99503
(907) 561-5135

ADVENTURE STARTS HERE

Whitewater rafting— World class mountain climbing— Walk or jet boat right up to a glacier— Superb X-C skiing— Terrific salmon fishing— Dog sled adventures— Flightseeing and much more! Write or call for information.

MATANUSKA-SUSITNA
CONVENTION & VISITORS BUREAU

P.O. Box 875747, Dept. B
Wasilla, AK 99687
Phone: (907) 376-8000

Nome Convention and Visitors Bureau. Box 251, Nome, AK 99762. (907) 443-5535.

Sitka Convention and Visitors Bureau. 330 Harbor Drive, Sitka, AK 99835. (907) 747-5940.

Skagway Convention and Visitors Bureau. Box 415, Skagway, AK 99840. (907) 983-2854.

Valdez Convention and Visitors Bureau. (See advertisement this page). Box 1603-AV, Valdez, AK 99686. (907) 835-2984.

Valdez. Get away to it all!

Fish for salmon and halibut in the waters of Prince William Sound.

Hike back into history to discover a famous Gold Stamp Mill.

Ride a river raft down magnificent Keystone Canyon.

Hear the echoes of the past at our Heritage Center Museum.

And listen to the stillness inside yourself.

You can drive, fly, or sail to Valdez 365 days a year.

Experience the untamed grandeur of Alaska, in a very civilized setting.

Valdez.

For vacation planning information, write or call the Valdez Convention and Visitors Bureau, Box 1603-AV, Valdez, AK 99686; (907) 835-2984.

**Winter Carnival
March 18-22**

**Gold Rush Days
July 8-12**

VALDEZ
ALASKA